INSIGHT COMPACT GUIDE

SOU
Spain

GW00367818

Compact Guide: Southern Spain is the ultimate quick-reference guide to this popular holiday destination. It tells you all you need to know about the region's attractions, from the Moorish magnificence of Córdoba and Granada to the scenic beauty of the Sierra Nevada, from the glitzy delights of Marbella and the Costa del Sol to the alleyways of Cádiz.

This is one of 130 Compact Guides, combining the interests and enthusiasms of two of the world's best known information providers: Insight Guides, whose titles have set the standard for visual travel guides since 1970, and Discovery Channel, the world's premier source of nonfiction television programming.

APA PUBLICATIONS
Part of the Langenscheidt Publishing Group

Insight Compact Guide: Southern Spain

Written by: Susanne Asal
English version by: Paul Fletcher
Edited by: Pam Barrett
Photography by: Jerry Dennis and Mark Read
Cover picture by: PowerStock/Zefa
Design: Tanvir Virdee
Picture Editor: Hilary Genin
Design concept: Carlotta Junger
Maps: Polyglott

Editorial Director: Brian Bell
Managing Editor: Tony Halliday

CONTACTING THE EDITORS: As every effort is made to provide accurate information in this publication, we would appreciate it if readers would call our attention to any errors and omissions by contacting:
Apa Publications, PO Box 7910, London SE1 1WE, England.
Fax: (44 20) 7403 0290
e-mail: insight@apaguide.demon.co.uk

Information has been obtained from sources believed to be reliable, but its accuracy and completeness, and the opinions based thereon, are not guaranteed.

© 2002 APA Publications GmbH & Co. Verlag KG Singapore Branch, Singapore.

First Edition 2002
Printed in Singapore by Insight Print Services (Pte) Ltd
Original edition © Polyglott-Verlag Dr Bolte KG, Munich

Worldwide distribution enquiries:
APA Publications GmbH & Co. Verlag KG (Singapore Branch)
38 Joo Koon Road, Singapore 628990
Tel: (65) 865-1600, Fax: (65) 861-6438

Distributed in the UK & Ireland by:
GeoCenter International Ltd
The Viables Centre, Harrow Way, Basingstoke,
Hampshire RG22 4BJ
Tel: (44 1256) 817987, Fax: (44 1256) 817-988

Distributed in the United States by:
Langenscheidt Publishers, Inc.
46–35 54th Road, Maspeth, NY 11378
Tel: (1 718) 784-0055, Fax: (1 718) 784-0640

www.insightguides.com

SOUTHERN SPAIN

Introduction

Top Ten Sights 4
Bridging East and West..7
Historical Highlights..18

Places

1 Seville 23
2 Córdoba 38
3 Granada..47
4 Spain's sunshine coast 58
5 Mediterranean to Atlantic...66
6 White villages of the sierras 75
7 Across Andalusia..80
8 Along the Guadalquivir 88
9 Across the Cordillera Bética...94

Culture

Art and Architecture..103
Literature 106
Flamenco 108
Festivals...109

Travel Tips

Food and Drink..113
Active Holidays...116
Practical Information...117
Accommodation 123

Index...128
Useful Phrases...................................Inside back cover

▷ **Antequera (p85)**
The lovely small town of Antequera typifies the Andalusian landscape; whitewashed houses clinging to the slopes of hills, the formal gardens of villas and palaces, a legacy of Islamic rule, and the expansive, sun-bleached vistas.

△ **Jerez (p88)**
Wherever you go in Jerez you will see the *bodegas* (cellars) of the large sherry producers, most of which offer tours.

△ **Cave Houses (p82)**
More than 2,000 cave dwellings can be found in and around Guadix and Purullena.

◁ **Beaches**
The Costa del Sol, though popular and crowded, still has some secluded spots.

◁ **Seville (p23)**
The Royal Palace, started in the 12th century and considered by many to be the finest Mudéjar palace in Spain, is only one of Seville's attractions. It is also a great place to hear traditional flamenco.

△ Granada (p47)
Home to the fabulous palace and gardens of the Alhambra, and home of Lorca, Granada's other treasures include its cathedral and the atmospheric alleys of the Albaicín quarter.

◁ Ronda (p75)
The town of Ronda is set on the spectacular El Tajo gorge and has the oldest bullring in Spain (1784).

▷ Almería (p58)
Almería is dominated by the massive walls of the 11th-century fortress.

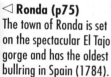

▽ Málaga (p61)
Much more than an entry point to the Costa del Sol, Málaga has a vibrant cultural life. Picasso was born here and many of his works are housed in the Casa Natal de Picasso.

◁ Córdoba (p38)
La Mezquita is Córdoba's centrepiece — an immense mosque built between the 8th and 10th centuries, with a cathedral in the middle of the prayer hall, standing out amid the Islamic architecture

Bridging East and West

The face of Andalusia has been shaped by the intermingling of various ethnic groups and the close proximity of North Africa. The Moorish inheritance is still very much in evidence, even though the influence of the Catholic Church has been paramount since the 15th century. To the casual observer it is sometimes difficult to distinguish between the two cultures. What is Arabic, what is Spanish? At different times, two of the south's important cities have controlled almost half the world: Córdoba in the 10th century and Seville in the 16th and 17th centuries – the first as an Islamic base in the west, the other as the main port for trade with the American colonies.

Opposite: the Alcazaba (fortress) in Almería
Below: Reales Alcazares in Seville
Bottom: cycling through Cazorla

INFLUENCES AND OBSESSIONS

Exquisite Renaissance, extravagant baroque and progressive decay have stamped an unmistakable character on the major cities. In the countryside a church and an *alcazaba* (Moorish castle) can often be seen standing next to each other, proudly symbolising the region's key cultural influences.

Listening to the *cante jondo*, the sound of true flamenco, with its mournful guitar and stamping heels, tells you there is something special about the people. Muslim influences, engendering a fatalistic view of life, historically marred by poverty, and an obsession with death, are all facets of the modern Andalusian character. But to compensate, *andaluces* are always keen to enjoy themselves. *Fiestas*, *romerías* and *carnavales* reflect their determination to enjoy life to the full. To keep the celebrations flowing, delicious *tapas* – one of several culinary delights bequeathed to the world by the Andalusians – are washed down with a glass of traditional *fino* (dry Jerez sherry).

SITUATION AND GEOGRAPHY

Spanish historian, Salvador de Madariaga, once said that Spain is a castle, separated from the rest of Europe by the natural barrier of the Pyrenees.

Nature's Contrasts
Natural wonders abound. The mighty Guadalquivir, a vital source of water, crosses the region from its source in the Sierra Cazorla, flowing into the sea by the beaches and *marismas* of the Coto Doñana National Park, a vast wildlife sanctuary. To the east are the peaks of the Sierra Nevada, snow-capped for most of the year. This mountain range is only 30 km (18 miles) from the Costa Tropical where sugar cane thrives.

Olive groves on the slopes of the Cazorla National Park near Jaen

But Andalusia is cut off from the north by another natural obstacle, the vast Sierra Morena between the Meseta Central plateau and Andalusia.

The land area of Andalusia is 87,268 sq.km (33,694 sq.miles), representing 17 percent of the Spanish mainland. Three major geographical features dominate the region. Below the 600-km (375-mile) long Sierra Morena mountain range is the Guadalquivir valley, a vital artery. Near Ubeda, the upper river valley is only 10km (6 miles) wide, but it opens out to a breadth of 300km (185 miles) as it flows into the Atlantic. The valley, with an average height of only 100m (330ft), forms a triangle between the Sierra Morena and the Cordillera Bética, the third of the three main features. It consists of the Sierras Subbéticas in the north and the Cordillera Penibética further south where Monte Mulhacén (3,478m/ 11,408ft), the highest mountain in the Iberian peninsula, dominates the Sierra Nevada. The valley between the two mountain ranges is the Surco Intrabético.

VARIED LANDSCAPES

The landscapes of Andalusia are surprisingly varied. Harsh mountain regions around Ronda alternate with farmland *(campiña)*; elsewhere desert regions give way to fertile plains *(vegas)*. It only takes two hours by car to get from Granada and the snow-capped mountains of the Sierra Nevada to the sunny Mediterranean coast.

The coastal strip, the Costa del Sol, has been blighted by holiday developments, but it is still an immensely popular holiday playground. A short way inland lie the timeless 'white villages', the primitive mountain settlements in the Alpujarras and the bizarre lunar landscapes of Almería's desert, much favoured by film-makers.

CLIMATE

Andalusia's climate is characterised by mild winters and long, hot summers. Between July and September the coastal temperature can soar to over 35°C (95°F), inland to at least 40°C (104°F). Between December and February the thermometer drops on average to about 12°C (53°F), but in the winter months on the Costa del Sol temperatures of 20°C (68°F) are common. Up in the mountains, however, it can get much colder. The wettest parts of the region are the provinces of Cádiz and Córdoba. The rainy seasons are autumn and spring. Snow falls only in the Sierra Nevada and the peaks remain white during late spring and early autumn.

WHEN TO GO

The best time to travel depends on the sort of holiday you are looking for. Sightseeing in the towns is not recommended during the summer months. The perfect place to be when the mercury rises is on the beach by the Atlantic coast, as a cool breeze often blows in off the sea. The mild winters on the Costa del Sol attract long-stay visitors from chilly northern Europe, but spring and autumn offer the best conditions for a holiday. From mid-September to early November and from March to early June, you can swim, walk, surf, go sightseeing, learn the language or tour the countryside on horseback, without fear of sunburn or frostbite. There is only one time of the year, however, to see nature at its most colourful and

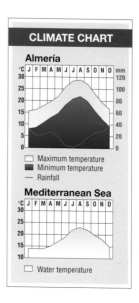

CLIMATE CHART

Almería

Mediterranean Sea

□ Maximum temperature
■ Minimum temperature
— Rainfall

□ Water temperature

Tarifa beach

that, of course, is spring. Fields of corn, poppies, sunflowers, cotton and fallow land, cork oak forests, olive and orange groves create every imaginable hue.

Natural Treasures

The true treasures of Andalusia lie well away from the coast. It is easy to imagine that the region is nothing but built-up coastlines with modern holiday settlements or hectare after hectare of plastic-covered greenhouses *(invernaderos)* for growing fruit and vegetables all the year round, but try exploring the hinterland and you will get a pleasant surprise.

The vegetation is predominantly Mediterranean with woodland consisting of leathery, evergreen foliage such as chestnuts, carob trees and pines, and the *dehesa* landscape of holm oaks and cork oaks, whose acorns nurture the Iberian pig, the animal that produces delicious and much-valued hams. Macchia scrub (*matorral* in Spanish) of thyme and myrtle cover many slopes. Some 4,000 different plants thrive in Andalusia, including about 150 endemic plants – species found nowhere else on earth.

Elsewhere there are the towering sierras, a dramatic background for colonies of vultures, peregrine falcons and eagle owls.

Below: bougainvillea in Málaga
Bottom: the Sierra Nevada from Granada

GUARDING THE ENVIRONMENT

Centuries of farming have sadly destroyed many natural habitats and it is only in recent years that politics has started to play a part in man's relationship to the environment. About 20 percent of land is now protected as a nature reserve *(reserva natural)* or nature park *(parque natural)*. The Parque Nacional Coto de Doñana in Andalusia, the nature reserve between Sanlúcar de Barrameda and Matalascañas, is one of the largest in Europe and has a unique balance between marshland *(marisma)* and bush. About two-thirds of it is marsh- and wetlands. The land was owned by the dukes of Medina Sidonia and was spared human intervention for centuries because it was used exclusively for hunting. The variety of fauna to be found here is extraordinary. It is an important bird reserve, a breeding ground for about 100 species and a place where thousands of European migratory birds break their journey or overwinter.

As well as the Coto de Doñana there are 22 other nature reserves where fauna and flora enjoy government protection. The Spanish National Tourist Office *(see page 120)* can supply information leaflets on the various parks.

> **Rural Tourism**
> As in other parts of Spain, a heightened awareness of and interest in the environment has led to a scheme called Turismo Rural. Farmhouses and cottages offer bed & breakfast or self-catering accommodation to people who want to spend their holidays birdwatching, walking, or even painting the landscape. For details, contact Red Andaluz de Alojamientos Rurales, Apartado 2035, 04080 Almería.

HUMAN ERROR

However, the region is a notable example of how mankind has failed the environment. The holiday villages and the water-intensive rice and strawberry farming on the fringes of the national park have already caused lasting damage as the water table has dropped dramatically. When 5 million cubic metres (180 million cubic feet) of heavily polluted water escaped from a fractured storage reservoir belonging to a mining company near Aznalcóllar in April 1998, the toxic chemicals contaminated thousands of hectares of farmland as well as the water courses that feed the marshland. A series of special measures forming part of the Doñana 2005 project should restore the sensitive ecosystem.

The attractive water features in the towns, the golf courses, even the flood-lit tennis courts, are

Strawberry picking in the Alpujarras

> ### Golden Vintage
> A chunk of land in the west of the province of Cádiz is known as the Golden Triangle. Here grow the grapes, mainly the Palomino variety, that produce sherry. The name, sherry, is simply an anglicised version of Jerez, the town where most of the production is concentrated.

Below: advert for sherry
Bottom: boat maintenance in Almería

also a considerable burden on Andalusia's natural resources. Tourism can seriously affect the delicate ecological balance. When guests at Costa del Sol hotels take too many showers during periods of drought it can result in local people having their water turned off in the evening.

THE ECONOMY

Together with Extremadura, Andalusia, which is home to some 6 million people, has the lowest per capita income in the country and the highest unemployment rate, at 30 percent (20.9 percent for the whole of Spain). Illiteracy levels in the region are also high – 11 percent compared to 4 percent nationally.

Andalusia is a region that continues to be dominated by agriculture, even if its importance is now waning. Some 22 percent of Spain's produce is grown here and farming still provides employment for 20 percent of the working population. Cereals, olive oil and wine make up a large part of the yield, but sunflowers, sugar beet, citrus fruit, cotton and tobacco are also grown. Apart from the coastal valleys near Málaga and Almería, most farms are owned by large landowners.

Industry has made little headway in these parts. About 85 percent of Andalusia's industrial goods come from northern Spain or abroad. The most important industry in Andalusia is mining. Steel production, primarily for the shipyards in Cádiz, is well established in Huelva and Cádiz, while chemicals are processed in Huelva and Algeciras. All the other industry is engendered by the region's agricultural products: sugar production in Cádiz and Granada, olive oil pressing around Jaén and the production of wine and sherry in Jerez, Córdoba and Montilla. In Huelva and Cádiz the fishing industry and fish canning are an important part of the economy.

The service sector – trade, transport and tourism – now employs 52 percent of the working population, and is responsible for over half of total output. Some 14 percent of Spain's tourist industry is based in Andalusia.

ADMINISTRATION

Andalusia's cultural identity has never been in doubt and it was never one of Madrid's political objectives to sever ties with the region. A paper written by Blas Infante in 1915 and entitled *El ideal andaluz* was the first manifestation of any Andalusian regional awareness. It was not until the mid-1960s that a movement in favour of greater regional autonomy won genuine popular support. The focus of discontent was deprivation in the rural community and anger was directed at centralist rule from Madrid, but was not heeded during the dictatorship.

After the death of General Franco in 1975 calls for regional government were expressed more openly, and Andalusians voted strongly in favour of autonomous status in the 1980 referendum. The region was then on course for a good measure of independence from Madrid.

For many years Andalusia was a Socialist stronghold. In 1994, however, the Socialist Party (PSOE) lost seats to the right-wing Partido Popular and the Izquierda Unida (United Left), but still clung on to power. Seville is the seat of the parliament and the regional government. Andalusia breaks down into 8 provinces: Seville, Cádiz, Huelva, Córdoba, Granada, Jaén, Málaga and Almería. Every province has its own administrative organ, the Diputación Provincial.

The art of pouring sherry

GITANOS

When the flamenco star, Joaquín Cortés, appears on stages throughout the world, his fans squabble over admission tickets, while critics applaud his athletic techniques. Arriving on stage with a bare chest, the long-haired dancer has become a new sex symbol throughout Spain. But for Joaquín Cortés, the fact that as a *gitano* he is winning such public acclaim is far more important. This is something that he emphasises every time he speaks: 'If I can give respect to my people, then that is a great benefit.'

But Cortés has set himself a difficult task. He belongs to the same minority (there are between 500,000 and 700,000 in the country) as the women who offer rosemary twigs to reluctant visitors outside Granada cathedral.

A DISCRIMINATED PEOPLE

Gypsies in southern Spain, as in many other parts of the world, are regarded as outcasts. Ever since they left their homeland in India during the 13th century and crossed Africa and Asia to reach Europe, they have been despised as vagabonds and treated with hostility. In Spain, where they settled in the 15th century, they were subjected to intolerance until well into the 18th century. They suffered persecution and ill-treatment just like the Moors and Jews. In 1539 Felipe II ordered all homeless *gitanos* to be taken on as galley slaves. On 20 July 1749, 12,000 gypsies were murdered in Spain as part of a barbaric pogrom. Discrimination against *gitanos* continues to this day.

The standing of Spanish gypsies, who call themselves *calé*, is ambivalent. Spanish culture has benefited greatly from their artistry. No singer or dancer can interpret flamenco as convincingly as a *gitano*. It is, after all, the way their ancestors have expressed themselves for hundreds of years. But their position in society is diametrically opposed to their prestige as artists. In southern Spain, gypsies are banished to their own quarters, for example in Tarifa and Almería. Unemployment is high among *gitanos* partly due

Romantic Views

Gitanos have often fared a lot better in literature and opera than in real life. Federico García Lorca wrote a series of gypsy ballads, *Romancero gitano*, in the 1920s; and Prosper Merimée's *Carmen*, written in 1845 and popularised by Bizet's opera, has given us one of the most enduring images of a sultry and passionate woman.

Gitano woman in Granada

to distrust and prejudice on the part of potential employers, and partly to the fact that their educational achievements are lower.

ANCIENT TRADITIONS

Gitanos are determined to preserve their cultural traditions, including their choice of abode, their own medicines and the hierarchical structure within their clans. A programme of integration introduced by the PSOE was well-meaning, but bore little fruit, as many of those it was meant to help chose not to participate.

Centuries of alienation have led to the formation of an authoritarian hierarchy demanding obedience from its members to the council of elders. In a modern democracy such a system is seen as anachronistic and hostile to women. But without such strong patriarchal structures it is doubtful that the *gitano* community would be able to endure the constant contempt and discrimination.

FLAMENCO

Flamenco is a legacy of Spain's distant Arabic past, but it has also picked up some gypsy traditions and Jewish/Hebrew elements on the way. Hovering around one note, singing several notes for a single syllable, and using scales with

Below: a flamenco performance in Córdoba
Bottom: dressed for flamenco in Ronda

Below: flamenco in tiles in Marbella
Bottom: matador statue in Ronda

intermediate notes are all alien to Western harmonies. Flamenco emerged from the poorest quarters of Ronda, Seville and Cádiz as a cry for help, a response to alienation and the suppression of the gypsies, peasants and Moriscos (Muslims forcibly converted to Christianity on pain of death). It is a song of pain, of deep emotion, of desperation, and of rebellion.

Initially, flamenco was only sung in private or in small bars, known as *juergas*. Dancing developed out of the songs. Originally, they were accompanied only by *palmas*, rhythmic handclapping. When, during the 1920s, flamenco was seen as ripe for the stage, it had to drop its hard edge and defiance, qualities which stood in the way of commercial appeal. The song-and-dance performances in the *cafés cantantes* soon became popular throughout all stratas of society.

As its audience grew, it added choreographed sequences and was performed in *tablaos,* aficionados' bars. But these had little to do with the *cante jondo* of pure flamenco, the 'singing from the depths', or *duende*, when the performer experiences a profound and mysterious immersion in the emotions of the music or dance. The best opportunities to see genuine flamenco arise if you are in the region for the *Semana Santa* processions, the week before Easter, in which gypsies take part, or for the *Burlería* flamenco festival at Jerez de la Frontera in September.

BULLFIGHTING

Nowhere in Spain is bullfighting taken more seriously than in Andalusia. There can be no *feria* – the annual fiesta – without a *corrida*. Exhibition fights against wild bulls, staged in the style of a knights' tournament, were originally the privilege of the Spanish nobility. When, towards the end of the 18th century, court society decided to copy the costumes and customs of the people, the dangerous sport of bullfighting on foot – as it was conducted by commoners – became acceptable.

Special arenas (*plazas de toros*) were built, rules were set for how the fight would proceed and books were written about it. The splendid costumes the bullfighters wear are based on the fashions existing at the time of Goya (1746–1828).

Despite the bad press it receives elsewhere, bullfighting, the *corrida de toros*, is still hugely popular in Spain. During the season, which lasts from March to October, television and newspapers give detailed reports on the fights. The battle between human intellect and animal instinct makes for a compelling spectacle, although it almost invariably ends in the death of the bull.

BREEDING FOR BUSINESS

The bulls, bred specially for the fight, spend 3–5 years in the meadow, before arriving at the arena. They must weigh at least 400 kilos (880lbs).

Bullfighting is big business. It is subject largely to the control of managers, who hire the arenas, buy the bulls, organise ticket sales and employ the *toreros*. What bullfighters earn is dependent on their category and on the rank of the arena. The leading figures are millionaires. Current favourite is Espartaco Jesús Janeiro (Jesulín de Ubrique), who set a world record in 1994 after taking part in 153 *corridas*.

Women had no place in the arena until 1974, when Cristina Sánchez broken into a world that hitherto had been reserved for males.

'Suit of lights' in Córdoba's Bullfighting Museum

HISTORICAL HIGHLIGHTS

Prehistory Skeletons of Neanderthal Man from the Old Stone Age have been found in Gibraltar and Nerja. Evidence of human habitation during Neolithic era and Bronze Age in Almería province.

circa 1000BC Phoenicians found Gadir (Cádiz) on the Atlantic and Mediterranean trading posts, including Malaka (Málaga). They introduce writing and money.

700–3000BC Carthage captures Málaga, Almuñécar and Adra.

206BC After the Second Punic War, the Romans control Iberian peninsula.

1st century AD Roman province of Baetica (Andalusia) makes significant contributions in food and wealth to the empire. Cities such as Acinipo, near Ronda, are built. Aqueducts and the theatre in Málaga are constructed.

2nd century Trade develops along the southern coast. Settlers include Syrians, Greeks, Romans, Hebrews and north Africans. Christianity quickly takes hold.

First half of 5th century Roman Empire in decline. Germanic Alani and Vandal tribes spread through southern Spain.

First half of 6th century Visigoths established, with Toledo as the capital of their empire, which extends across almost all the Iberian peninsula. In 586 they adopt Catholicism.

711 Tariq, an Arabic colonel, enters Gibraltar. This marks the beginning of the Muslim invasion.

8th century The Moorish empire extends as far as the Pyrenees. In 718 Christians attack the Moors at Covadonga (Asturias). The long *Reconquista* (Reconquest) begins.

756–1031 Damascene Umayyads rule in al-Andalus. Art and science flourish; the guitar is invented. Sugar cane, herbs and spices, and fruits such as oranges, lemons and apricots, are introduced into the region.

929 Abd ar-Rahman III becomes caliph; his city, Córdoba, becomes the European seat of culture and learning.

1031 The Caliphate fragments into 26 independent kingdoms *(taifas)*. The south coast becomes part of the province of Granada.

1081–85 Alfonso VI conquers Toledo. Taifas ask the Almoravids for support.

1090–1145 The Moorish empire unites under the Almoravids. They prove to be harsh rulers who push back the Christians and subjugate the Al-Andalus.

1146–1236 The Almohads defeat the Almoravids and make Seville their capital. They are more tolerant, encourage learning and construct fine buildings.

1212 Christians defeat the Almohads at Las Navas de Tolosa. Soon other Muslim centres are captured by Christians.

1238 The armies of Nasrid Mohammed Ibn al-Ahmar capture the Mediterranean coast from Gibraltar to Almería. Nasrid kingdom is established in Granada. Under the rule of Mohammed ibn Jusuf ibn Nasr, work commences on the Alhambra Palace.

1246 Nasrids submit to Ferdinand III of Castile. Their kingdom continues as a vassal state for 250 years.

1462 Castilian troops capture Gibraltar from the Moors.

1469 Isabela of Castile and Ferdinand of Aragón, the Catholic Monarchs, marry, uniting the two largest kingdoms in Spain; they begin the Inquisition.

1487 Málaga falls to Christians and the town's importance begins to wane.

1492 The last fortification in Granada relinquished without a fight. Persecution of the Jews begins. Christopher Columbus reaches America.

1502 Muslims offered forcible conversion or expulsion. The majority are baptised (the so-called Moriscos).

1516 Under Carlos V, Spain becomes a major power.

1523 Building of Granada's cathedral begins, under Enrique Egas.

1528 Building of Málaga cathedral starts and lasts 250 years.

1600 Spain's Golden Age with Andalusian painters and sculptors such as Velázquez, Murillo and Alonso Cano making their mark.

1609 Felipe III expels the Moriscos.

1701–14 The War of Spanish Succession. Gibraltar captured by the British in 1704, and is ceded to Britain in perpetuity under the Treaty of Utrecht in 1713.

1805 Admiral Nelson defeats Spanish-French fleet off Cape Trafalgar.

1808 French troops occupy Spain; Napoleon replaces the Spanish king with his brother, Joseph Bonaparte. The subsequent War of Independence lasts until 1814.

1812 Liberal constitution proclaimed in Cádiz, but rejected by Fernando VII.

1859–60 War against Morocco.

1873 Proclamation of Spain's First Republic.

1923–30 Military dictatorship under Miguel Primo de Riveras.

1931 Proclamation of the Second Republic. The king goes into exile.

1936–39 At least 600,000 Spaniards die in the Spanish Civil War. When the Falangists emerge as winners, Franco imposes a dictatorship.

1960s Mass tourism begins to hit the beaches of the Costa del Sol.

1975 Death of Franco. Spain becomes a constitutional monarchy.

1977 The first free election is held.

1981 Andalusia attains autonomy, with its own president and parliament.

1982 Felipe González is elected as prime minister.

1986 Spain joins the EC.

1992 Seville hosts Expo '92. Investment pours into Andalusia.

1994 Socialists lose absolute majority in Spanish Parliament.

1996 Partido Popular under José María Aznar comes to power.

1998 Centenary of the birth of Federico García Lorca.

2002 From March the Euro replaces the peseta as Spain's main currency.

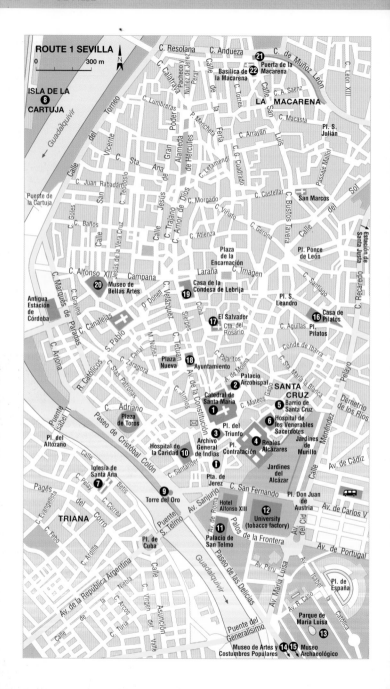

ROUTE 1 SEVILLA
0   300 m
N

ISLA DE LA
CARTUJA ⑧

LA MACARENA

㉑ Puerta de la Macarena
㉒ Basílica de la Macarena
Pl. S. Julián
San Marcos
Pl. Ponce de León
Estación de Santa Justa
Pl. S. Leandro
⑯ Casa de Pilatos
Pl. Pilatos

Guadalquivir

Puente de la Cartuja

Plaza de la Encarnación

⑳ Museo de Bellas Artes

Antigua Estación de Córdoba

⑲ Casa de la Condesa de Lebrija

⑰ El Salvador

⑱ Plaza Nueva

Ayuntamiento

Palacio Arzobispal ②

Catedral de Santa María ①

SANTA CRUZ

⑤ Barrio de Santa Cruz

⑥ Hospital de los Venerables Sacerdotes

Pl. del Triunfo

③ Archivo General de Indias

⑩ Hospital de la Caridad

④ Reales Alcázares

Pl. Contratación

Jardines de Murillo

Jardines del Alcázar

Plaza de Toros

Pl. del Altozano

Iglesia de Santa Ana ⑦

TRIANA

⑨ Torre del Oro

Pta. de Jerez

Hotel Alfonso XIII

C. San Fernando

Pl. Don Juan de Austria

Av. de Carlos V

⑫ University (tobacco factory)

Pl. de Cuba

⑪ Palacio de San Telmo

Av. de Portugal

Av. Peru

Guadalquivir

Puente del Generalísimo

Parque de María Luisa ⑬

Pl. de España

Museo de Artes y Costumbres Populares ⑭ ⑮ Museo Arqueológico

1: Seville

Map on page 22

Of the three major cities in Andalusia, Seville, its capital, set on the banks of the Guadalquivir, is the star. The fourth largest city in Spain, with about 700,000 inhabitants, it is the seat of government for the autonomous region and its university is the most important in Andalusia. The vast Gothic Cathedral and the magnificent Alcázar lord it over the city. In the Santa Cruz *barrio* (quarter), there are shady courtyards and Sevillian *carmens* (villas enclosing a patio), wafting flamenco music, and the smell of orange blossom in the spring.

It is also in spring that the dramatic processions of *Semana Santa* (Holy Week) and the exuberance of the *Feria* (in April) draw thousands to the city, from the surrounding region and far beyond.

Sacred and Secular

Semana Santa in Seville is unmatched for religious spectacle. Huge, ornate floats portraying scenes from the Passion are carried through the streets, accompanied by men in hooded costumes.

The April *Feria* is a secular occasion when parades of gorgeously clad *Sevillanos*, on horseback or in open carriages, file through Los Remedios district, and a giant funfair takes over the streets.

HISTORY

The Romans called it Hispalis, the Moors adorned it with mosques and palaces, but Seville's 'Golden Age' began with the discovery of the New World. In 1503, the Casa de la Contratación (House of Trade) was founded by Queen Isabela I, assuring Seville of its trading monopoly with overseas territories. In the 16th century it was the richest city in Spain. Duties on all imports from the Americas had to be paid on arrival at the riverside port. Gold and silver from the colonies poured in, financing extravagant buildings and equally extravagant lifestyles until, around 1700, the Río Guadalquivir began to silt up, preventing large vessels from reaching the inland port.

When, in 1778, the liberal economic policies of the Bourbon rulers led to the lifting of the monopoly on trade with the Americas, Seville's commercial decline began. It was to continue for more than two centuries.

In the last decade of the 20th century, Expo '92, a giant celebration of Columbus's voyage to the Americas 500 years earlier, saw major investment in the city's infrastructure, designed to accelerate progress. To what extent the city benefited is something that Sevillanos are still questioning.

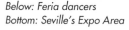
Below: Feria dancers
Bottom: Seville's Expo Area

Maps
on pages
22 & 25

Plateresque
Plateresque is one of the lesser-known architectural terms. It refers to the early period of Spanish Renaissance building when the intricate ornamentation was likened to the work of a silversmith – a *platero*.

Below: sculpture detail on the Puerta Mayor
Bottom: the Cathedral in all its glory

CENTRAL SIGHTS

The ★★★ **Catedral de Santa María ❶** (Monday to Saturday, 10.30am–5pm, Sunday 2–6pm) is listed in the *Guinness Book of Records* as the third largest church in the world (after St Paul's in London and St Peter's in Rome).

Like many churches in the region, Seville Cathedral started out as a mosque. Work on the foundation walls began under the Almohads in 1402, and most of the main structure was built over the next 100 years. The two 15th-century portals flanking the **Puerta Mayor ❹** are of interest: on the right is the **Puerta del Nacimiento** (Nativity), to the left the **Puerto del Bautismo** (Baptism). From the same era, and opening on to the Calle de los Alemanes, is the **Puerta del Perdón ❸**, the Gate of Forgiveness, later ornamented in plateresque style.

Behind it lies the **Patio de los Naranjos ❻**, Patio of the Orange Trees, originally the mosque's courtyard where the ritual ablutions took place (access via a gate near the Giralda). The marble basin of the fountain is of Visigothic origin.

The **Puerta de la Concepción ❹** is an early 20th-century addition. In front of the **Puerta del Lagarto ❺**, a wooden crocodile recalls the unsuccessful request by an Egyptian sultan for the hand of Alfonso X's daughter.

SYMBOL OF THE CITY

The ★★**Giralda** is not just a symbol for Seville, it is also a simple and beautiful feature that blends in harmoniously with the rest of the cathedral complex. Begun in 1184 by the Almohads as a minaret, the Giralda was turned into a bell tower by the Christians. Work began on the balconies and spire in 1558. The bronze figure crowning the 94-m (308-ft) high structure, an emblem of Christian faith, serves as a weathervane, hence its name which derives from the Spanish word *giraldillo* (*girar* means to turn). The climb to the top via series of ramps is easy.

The Capilla Real, flanked by two portals, forms the cathedral's east side. Depicted in the tympanum of the **Puerta de los Palos** Ⓖ is the Adoration of the Three Kings; in the same position in the **Puerta de las Campanillas** is a rendering of Christ entering Jerusalem.

The Giralda

INTERIOR FEATURES

Enter the cathedral through the **Puerta del Lagarto**. Stand at the crossing and look westwards toward the choir, where the 16th-century grille stands out as a masterpiece of Spanish craftsmanship. The carved and gilded high altar in the presbytery is the largest in the world. Over 200 sacred figures adorn the *retablo*. Pieter Dancart began the task in 1482, but it was 100 years before the whole project was completed.

Behind the high altar lies the **Capilla Real** Ⓗ (Royal Chapel), which was renovated in Renaissance style during the 16th century. In a silver sarcophagus in front of the altar lie the mortal remains of Fernando III, the since-canonised ruler who captured Seville from the Moors in 1248. On the walls are the tombs of his wife, Beatrice of Swabia and his son Alfonso X, the Wise. A processional monstrance by Juan de Arfe (16th century) and Zurbarán's *St Theresa* can be seen in the **Sacristía Mayor** Ⓘ.

CATHEDRAL

Maps on pages 22 & 25

The **Tomb of Christopher Columbus** ❿ was brought to Seville cathedral in 1902. Figures representing the kingdoms of Spain hold the coffin aloft so that it does not touch the floor – Columbus did not wish to be buried in Spanish soil.

The striking painting in the **Capilla de San Antonio baptismal chapel** ⓚ is the *Vision of St Anthony in Padua* by Murillo (1617–82) .

Below: inside the Royal Palace
Bottom: decorative detail

AROUND THE CATHEDRAL

The 18th-century **Palacio Arzobispal** ❷ (Archbishop's Palace) by the Plaza de la Virgen de los Reyes has a splendid staircase and is a fine example of the baroque style. It is still used by the clergy of Seville.

At the other side of the cathedral, the two-storey **Lonja** (Stock Exchange) was built from 1583–98 in the severe style of Juan de Herreras, Felipe II's court architect. Since 1785 the building has housed the **Archivo General de Indias** ❸ (Monday to Friday 10am–1pm), where countless papers document relations between Spain and its American colonies.

THE ROYAL PALACE

The ★★★ **Reales Alcazares** ❹ (Tuesday to Saturday 9.30am–7pm, Sunday 9.30am–5pm, closed Monday; October to April, reduced opening

times) is regarded by many as the finest Mudéjar palace in Spain. Started in the 12th century during the Almohad era, it was taken over by Christians after the *Reconquista* (1248) and enlarged on several occasions until well into the 16th century. Much of the older part of the palace was built by King Pedro the Cruel (1350–69), who, among other things, lived up to his name by murdering some of his guests.

PATIOS AND SALONS

To enter the palace, you first cross the Patio de la Montería (Hunter's Patio) and the Patio del León (Lion Patio). At the south side of the latter, the main Puerta de León entrance is adorned with a tiled picture of a crowned lion.

Behind the main entrance, a narrow, angled passageway leads to the ★ **Patio de las Doncellas** (Maidens' Patio), one of the two courtyards around which the palace is grouped and once the focal point for courtly life. To the south lie the **Salón de Carlos V** and the **Salón del Techo de Felipe II** and beyond is the Alcázar's showpiece, the ★★ **Salón de los Embajadores**, (Ambassadors' salon, 1427), with its wooden dome and gilded star-like ornamentation symbolising heaven. Pass through the **Sala de Felipe II** to reach the small but evocative ★ **Patio de las Muñecas** (Dolls' Patio), where the rulers' private life was enacted. This in turn provides access to the Hall of the Catholic Monarchs, the Princes' Room and the bedchamber of the Moorish kings with its fine wooden ceiling.

The 16th-century **Palacio de Carlos V** is reached by following the covered walkway that leads off to the left of the Patio de la Montería and across the inner garden. Underneath the walkway are the baths of María Padilla, mistress of Pedro the Cruel. She was said to have had several lovers and men of the court lined up for the strangely erotic act of drinking her bathwater – all except one who excused himself on the grounds that 'having tasted the sauce, he might covet the partridge'. Inside the palace, the first grand hall

Star Attraction
• the Royal Palace

Moorish Artistry
Given its similarity with the Alhambra in Granada, it is thought that much of the ceramic and stucco ornamentation work on the Alcázar was carried out by Moorish architects and craftsmen from that city. Introduced by the Moors, the blue glazed tiles called *azulejos* adorn the walls and plinths and further embellish the inner courtyards and gardens.

Puerta de León

Map on page 22

is furnished with copies of Flemish tapestries glorifying Carlos V's conquest of Tunisia. The *azulejo* decorations in the next room and the **palace chapel** illustrate scenes from the New World.

Extending to the south of the palace lie the magnificent **Jardines de los Alcázares** with a wealth of exotic flora. Laid out in the 16th century, they have since been redesigned many times.

To avoid the long queues at the entrance kiosk, visit the Alcázar around midday when coach tours go for lunch.

Below: bar sign in the Barrio de Santa Cruz
Bottom: Jardines de los Alcázares

THE OLD JEWISH QUARTER

A passage to the south of the **Patio de las Banderas** (Patio of the Flags) leads to the Holy Cross district, ★★ **Barrio de Santa Cruz ❺**.

The narrow alleyways in the old Jewish quarter, the white facades, wrought-iron balconies, tiled inner courtyards and floral decorations evoke a genuine Andalusian atmosphere. Follow Calle Judería and Calle de la Vida to the finest square in this quarter, **Plaza de Doña Elvira**.

Nearby stands the **Hospital de los Venerables Sacerdotes ❻**, a home for infirm priests founded in 1675. Guided tours take in the delightful patio and the chapel housing some outstanding art works including frescoes by Juan de Valdés Leal and his son, Lucas Valdés.

Take Calles Reinoso and Lope de Rueda to the secluded **Plaza de Santa Cruz** where a late 17th-century wrought-iron cross adorns the centre.

It is hard to resist a stroll through the quarter, with its numerous shady plazas, countless restaurants, *tapas* bars and souvenir shops.

BY THE GUADALQUIVIR

The 19th-century **Puente de Isabel II** is a steel bridge across the Río Guadalquivir to the **Barrio de Triana**, a traditional working-class district that used to be the gypsy quarter. The view from the bridge encompasses the riverside promenade, the Torre del Oro and the nearby Plaza de Toros (bullfighting arena).

Triana is known for its pottery workshops and for its attractive white and ochre coloured buildings. The oldest church in the neighbourhood is the **Iglesia de Santa Ana ❼**. Begun in 1280, this building was given the baroque treatment during the 18th century. Muggings and robbery are not unheard off in this district, so be alert and carry only the bare essentials.

By way of contrast with the relative poverty of this quarter, the road leading along the south bank of the river, **Calle Betis**, is lined on both sides with a wide choice of smart and fairly expensive restaurants and bars.

A View of La Cartuja

Looking in the opposite direction towards **Isla de La Cartuja ❽** you will see the ultra-modern **Recinto de la Expo '92**, the site of the 1992 world trade fair. The **Pabellón de la Navegación** (Navigation Pavilion) has been retained as a permanent maritime museum (Tuesday to Sunday 10am–1pm, 5–8pm). The **Puente del Alamillo** by Santiago Calatrava, a respected Spanish architect, is a road bridge at the north end of the so-called island. The 142-m (466-ft) high pylon has become an important landmark and symbol of Seville. Calatrava's original design was for a symmetrical pair of bridges either side of La Cartuja,

Star Attraction
• Barrio de Santa Cruz

Magic Island
Isla Mágica is a theme park on the former Expo site. Open from 11 March to 1 November, it celebrates Columbus's voyages. Visitors find themselves transported back to the Seville of the 16th century and then experience an adventure in the New World. Monday to Thursday 11am– 9pm, Friday to Sunday, public holidays 11am–11pm; mid-June to mid-September, daily 11am–midnight; tel: 954 48 70 00.

Puente del Alamillo

Map on page 22

but only one of the two was built. The bridge's striking feature is its asymmetric design: its single pylon inclines away from the river, supporting the 200-m (655-ft) span with 13 pairs of cables. The weight of the concrete and steel pylon provides a counterbalance for the bridge deck.

Below: Plaza de Toros facade
Bottom: interior of the
Hospital de la Caritad

PASEO SIGHTS

From La Cartuja you can return via the Avenida Cristo de Expiración, or from Triana cross the modern Puente de San Telmo, to get back to Paseo de Colón on the north bank of the river. A stroll along this long, broad street leads past the impressive 18th-century **Plaza de Toros de las Real Maestranza** (Monday to Saturday 10am– 1.30pm). There is a museum here, and guided tours are available if you are interested in the history of the *corrida* but don't want to watch one. Nearby stands the new opera house, **Teatro de la Maestranza**, which opened in 1992.

The **Torre del Oro ❾**, the Golden Tower, was built by the Almohads in 1220 as a watchtower for the harbour. It was originally faced with golden tiles, the probable reason for its name, although it could also refer to the gold from the New World that was unloaded at the port. It now houses the **Museo Marítimo,** which is stuffed with fascinating odds and ends (Tuesday to

Friday 10am–1pm). Boat cruises on the river start from the tower.

Star Attraction
•**Hospital de la Caritad**

HOSPITAL DE LA CARIDAD

Cross the Paseo de Colón and head towards the city centre along Calle de Santander. On the left, on Calle Temprado, lies the ★★ **Hospital de la Caridad ⑩** (Monday to Saturday 9am–1.30pm, 3.30–6.30pm, Sunday/public holidays 9am–1pm; reduced opening times in winter), built to care for the old and the sick, a function it still performs today.

A fine example of 17th-century Sevillan baroque, it owes its foundation in 1674 to the Calatrava knight, Don Miguel de Mañara. Apparently Don Miguel, who had led a debauched existence, had a vision of his own funeral procession and immediately repented his past life, joined the Brotherhood of Charity and set up this hospital. It is said that Don Miguel provided the role model for the legend of Don Juan, the cynical lover who had 1,003 Spanish mistresses; however Tirso de Molina's book *El Burlador de Sevilla (The Seducer of Seville)*, based on the legend of Don Juan, was written in 1634.

The two-part courtyard behind the entrance is covered with Delft-blue tiles showing biblical scenes. The Seville artists, Bartolomé Esteban Murillo and Juan de Valdés Leal, were responsible for the paintings inside the hospital chapel Two of them, by Valdés Leal, demonstrating the transitory nature of life, are particularly morbid. The sculptor, Pedro Roldán, designed the high altar *retablo* in 1670. After the works in the Museo de Bellas Artes, the paintings here represent Seville's most important collection.

> **A fitting end**
> The story of Don Juan was a great one for Mozart to get his teeth into. His opera, *Don Giovanni*, first produced in Prague in 1787, tells the story of the 'Seducer of Seville' who, far from opening a home for the sick and needy, is eventually dragged down to hell by demons.

Delft tiles in the Hospital courtyard

BAROQUE PALACE

Paseo de las Delicias is the southern continuation of the Paseo de Colón. Continuing in this direction, you will come to the baroque **Palacio de San Telmo ⑪**, on the edge of San Telmo gardens. Once a maritime training school, later a seminary, it is now a government building.

Map on page 22

THE FACTORY WHERE CARMEN WORKED

Seville university's enormous faculty of science and law on Calle de San Fernando was once a **tobacco factory** ⓬. The building, designed by a military architect in 1725, was then the second-largest building in Spain after El Escorial. It housed the Real Fábrica de Tabacos, and was used as the setting for Prosper Merimée's tragic novella, *Carmen*.

Below: tobacco factory detail
Bottom: Parque de María Luisa

His heroine, who became far more widely known through Bizet's opera, came to represent the classic, sultry Andalusian temptress. Carmen supposedly worked in the factory, along with 3,000 other *cigarerras*, but nobody knows whether she was based on a real person or a composite of the women who worked in the factory when the author visited in 1840.

PARKS, PAVILIONS AND MUSEUMS

The adjoining ★ **Parque de María Luisa** ⓭ was given to the city by Infanta María Luisa. In 1929 the park was used for the 'Fair of the Americas' and some of the pavilions have survived.

A wide avenue extends as far as the ★★ **Plaza de España**, an impressive square and the site of the host country's pavilion. *Azulejo* scenes around the base of the semi-circle illustrate the history of the various provinces. Cross the Parque de María Luisa and you will come to Plaza de América where there are another three exhibition buildings.

Pabellón Mudéjar is now the home of the **Museo de Artes y Costumbres Populares** ⓮ (Art and Folklore Museum; Wednesday to Saturday 9am–8pm, Sunday/public holidays 9am–2.30pm, Tuesday/Thursday 3–8pm; October to April, reduced opening times). The displays here include furniture, costumes and everyday objects, as well as an interesting collection of *azulejos*.

Housed in the Pabellón Plateresco opposite is the **Museo Arqueológico** ⓯ (opening times as above). Artefacts exhibited here date from prehistoric times to the 15th century. Of special interest are the Carambolo Treasures (8th century BC) and finds from the Roman city of Itálica.

FURTHER SIGHTS

★★ Casa de Pilatos  (daily 9am–7pm) in Plaza de Pilatos, northeast of *barrio* Santa Cruz, is a privately owned palace displaying an unusual combination of styles, although Mudéjar is the dominant one. Rich stucco work adorns the main, two-storey courtyard. The tiling on the walls (1536–8) is of special interest as it attempts to imitate wall-hangings. Busts of Roman emperors occupy niches in the arcades. On the right is the **Salón del Pretorio**, which leads through into the **Jardín Chico**, the 'small garden'. The **Salón de la Fuente** on the left opens on to the **Jardín Grande**. A superb *artesonado* dome in the stairway is a miniature replica of the ceiling in the throne room at the Reales Alcázares.

Below: Casa de Pilatos
Bottom: Azulejo scenes
on Plaza de España

THE OLD AND THE NEW

From Plaza de Pilatos **Calle de las Águilas** leads to the pedestrian zone and to the late-baroque church of **El Salvador** , built on the site of Seville's first mosque. The harmonious interior is an impressive sight, while on the square outside the hustle and bustle of life in the city unfolds.

In the nearby Plaza Nueva stands the 16th-century **Ayuntamiento** ⓲ (Town Hall), a showpiece of plateresque style. The square is often used for open-air concerts.

Maps on pages 22 & 37

Shopping in Seville
If you want to buy designer clothes, try the local designers Victorio and Lucchino while you are in Calle Sierpes – they're at No. 87. For other shopping needs there are numerous handicrafts markets in the city – check at a tourist office for venues. If you are interested in ceramics and tiles there's the Santa Ana factory outlet in Triana, as well as several others pottery shops in this *barrio*.

To the north runs traffic-free **Calle Sierpes**, a shopper's paradise always bustling with activity. Gifts and souvenirs sold in the shops here include hand-painted fans, mantillas, porcelain, leather goods and haute couture.

In Calle Cuna, which runs parallel, stands the ★ **Casa de la Condesa de Lebrija** ⑲ (Monday to Friday 5–7pm; October to April reduced opening times), one of the few mansions in Seville open to the public. Built in the 16th century, it is particularly notable for its splendid decorative tiling. The rooms resemble Roman villas and the floor is covered with 3rd-century BC mosaics, which originate from nearby Itálica. If you are interested in Roman art, you simply must visit this palace. There is no better place to see the Itálica mosaics – neither the Archaeological Museum nor the ancient site itself has such a diverse collection.

MUSEUM OF FINE ARTS

From the Casa de Lebrija, Calle Alfonso XII runs straight to the ★★ **Museo de Bellas Artes** ⑳ (Wednesday to Saturday 9am–8pm, Sunday 9am–3pm). The art gallery is housed in the former Convento de la Merced, a well-restored 17th-century convent, and provides an excellent overview of southern Spanish art from the 15th

Bustling Calle Sierpes

century onwards. Of special importance is the large collection of baroque paintings from the Seville School, including works by Murillo and Juan de Valdés Leal.

LA MACARENA

Near the main bypass (Ronda de Sevilla or Calle Nuñoz León) in the north of the city stands the **Puerta de la Macarena ㉑**. On the left is the **Basílica de la Macarena ㉒** (Monday to Thursday 9am–1pm, 5–8pm; admission free), which was completed in 1949 after a fire destroyed the original. Above the high altar towers the much-revered Virgen de la Esperanza (17th century), known as La Macarena, which during Holy Week bears the jewels of the Duchess of Alba. Exhibited in the adjoining museum are the Virgin's costumes and jewellery and the *paso*, the bearer, on which the sacred icon is carried.

EXCURSIONS

Interesting excursions from Seville include visits to the Roman ruins at Itálica, two important nature reserves, and a trip to the Atlantic coast.

ROMAN REMAINS

Only 8km (5 miles) to the northwest of the city lie the ruins of ★ **Itálica** (Tuesday to Saturday 9am–8pm, Sunday 10am–4pm; October to April, reduced opening times). Founded in 206BC by Scipio Africanus, this is the oldest Roman settlement on Spanish soil and also the birthplace of the Roman emperors, Trajan and Hadrian. The **amphitheatre**, where there was seating for 25,000 spectators, is impressive. Starting just to the left of it is the **Cardo Maximus**, the main road through the town.

Wandering arounding the villa quarter (2nd century AD) it is still possible to make out the outlines of the dwellings and the mosaic floors, although many of the mosaics have been moved to the Archaeological Museum.

*Below: statue outside Itálica's amphitheatre
Bottom: mosaics at the Neptune House*

Map
on page
37

Virgen del Rocío

At Whitsuntide (late May) the sleepy village of El Rocío, with barely 1,000 inhabitants, is the scene of the largest and most spectacular pilgrimage in Spain. Pilgrims from the provinces of Huelva, Cádiz and Seville pour into El Rocío with decorated ox carts, on foot or on horseback to pay homage to the **Virgen del Rocío**, sometimes known as La Blanca Paloma (White Dove). A great deal of music, dancing, feasting and drinking are an essential part of the celebrations. If you are in Seville at this time and want to join in you should take the A49/E1 motorway in the direction of Huelva.

PARQUE NACIONAL COTO DE DONANA

The 'hunting grounds of Doña Ana' in the Guadalquivir delta once belonged to the dukes of Medina Sidonia. Nowadays, this area is noted for the wealth of its birdlife *(see page 11 for more details)*. The best way to explore the park is on an organised tour in a Land Rover (Monday to Saturday 8.30am–3pm). Group excursions last about 4 hours. Contact **Cooperativa Marismas del Rocío**, Almonte Huelva, about 12km (7 miles) along the Rocío–Matalascañas road (tel: 959 43 04 32; advance reservations recommended; approx. 2,700 ptas, but prices may change).

TO THE COAST AND THE MOUNTAINS

The final excursion takes you to the Atlantic coast and the Sierra de Aracena. Head westwards from Seville on the road to Huelva. After 65km (40 miles) you will be overwhelmed by the view of the village of **Niebla**, during the 11th century the capital of a tiny Moorish empire. The 3-km (2-mile) town wall with over 40 fortification towers has been meticulously restored.

Follow the Río Tinto towards **Moguer**. The town's most famous son is Juan Ramón Jiménez (1881–1958), the winner of the Nobel Prize for Literature in 1956. Although primarily a poet, Jiménez achieved popularity in America with the translation of his prose work *Platero y Yo* (1917), the story of a man and his donkey set in and around Moguer. His birthplace is now a museum (Monday to Saturday 10.15am–1.15pm, 5.15–7.15pm, Sunday mornings only).

About 5km (3 miles) from Moguer lies **Palos de la Frontera**, the starting point for Christopher Columbus's first voyage. The **San Jorge** church (1473) at the edge of the village has an interesting Mudéjar north portal.

Some 3km (2 miles) further on stands the 14th-century **Monasterio de la Rábida**, which also has connections with Columbus. On a journey from Portugal to La Rábida, he stopped here and talked to the influential abbot, Juan Pérez, who agreed to write to Queen Isabela on his behalf.

Moguer scene

SIERRA DE ARACENA

You can continue the excursion northwards into the ★ **Sierra de Aracena** nature reserve. The N435 runs right through the 3,000-sq.km (1,160-sq.mile) mountain region, which is covered mainly by oak and chestnut forests. The Atlantic climate strongly influences weather patterns in the southwestern foothills of the Sierra Morena, one of the wettest regions of Andalusia. The region's most famous export is *jamón jabugo*, an air-dried ham produced from the black Iberian pig, which feeds on acorns.

Aracena, 220km (136 miles) away, is the region's main town (pop. 6,300), and a very attractive spot. Perched on the highest hilltop are a Moorish castle and a church, the Iglesia del Castillo. Close by, the **Gruta de las Maravillas** is arguably the most impressive cave in Spain. Much of the film *Journey to the Centre of the Earth* was shot here.

Hams from the sierra

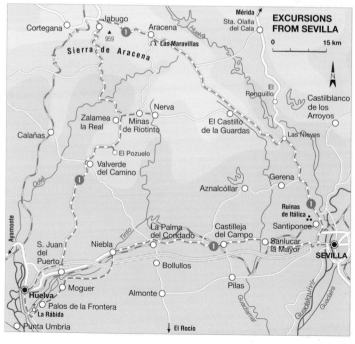

Map on page 39

Glory Days
During its heyday in the 10th century, Córdoba became a centre of advanced learning in sciences, medicine, philosophy and poetry. Together with Baghdad and Constantinople, it was one of the three great cities in the world. This at a time when parts of Europe were languishing in the Dark Ages.

Below: Córdoba veterans
Bottom: Mesquita facade

2: Córdoba

Córdoba (pop. 323,000) was the magnificent capital of the Cordoban Caliphate in the 10th century. Now it is a quiet provincial city by the Río Guadalquivir, the Arabic 'Great River' (Wadi al-Kebir), which flows through the fertile *campiña*.

It is thought that in its heyday the city was home to about half a million people, including Jewish and Christian minorities who were tolerated in the Islamic city. The nooks and crannies of the Old Town still reveal something of the atmosphere of medieval Córdoba. But the palaces and public baths, most of the mosques, the libraries and Koran schools, the caravanserais, studios and shops have disappeared. Fortunately the Great Mosque (the *Mezquita*) has survived the ravages of time. It is one of the most impressive Islamic cultural monuments in the world.

HISTORY

Córdoba, which probably owes its name to the Phoenicians, was an important administrative centre in Roman times. The settlement was conquered by the Moors in 712. When the Umayyad prince, Abd al-Rahman I, founded the Emirate of Córdoba in 756, the principal settlement in Al-Andalus was about to undergo a spectacular improvement in its fortunes. In 1031 the kingdom fell apart as a result of wrangling among the Umayyads. When the city was captured by Fernando III in 1236, he founded dozens of monasteries and went on to build numerous churches throughout the region.

The former layout of the Islamic city is still easy to make out. At its heart stood the main mosque. Dispersed around it is the market quarter. Extending as far as the city walls is the residential area and many of its narrow lanes and alleys can still be seen in the Old Town. Various trades with their own streets were clustered around the souk. Only tanners and potters were banished to the edge of town, the former probably because tanning is a smelly business, the latter is less easily explained.

SIGHTS

★★★ **La Mezquita** ❶ (spring to autumn, Monday to Saturday 10am–7.30pm, Sunday 2–7.30pm; reduced opening times from October), is the centrepiece of the Old Town, standing on the site of the original Visigothic San Vicente church. New sections were added during the Umayyads' reign. When the last piece was completed under

Star Attraction
•La Mezquita

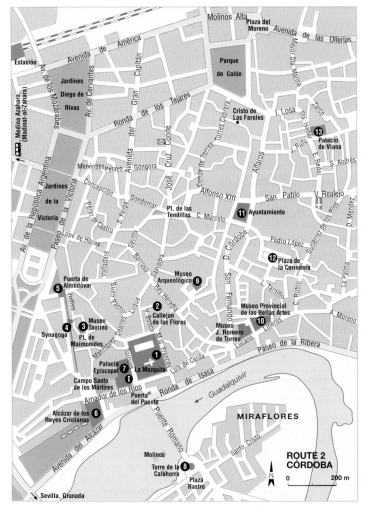

Maps on pages 39 & 40

Inside the Mezquita

Al-Mansur, it became the largest mosque in the western Islamic world. It is a typical example of a courtyard mosque, comprising a multi-nave prayer hall and forecourt. When the city was recaptured by the Christians in 1236, the mosque was initially used in its unaltered form as an episcopal church. During the 16th century, however, work began on a cathedral in the middle of the prayer hall, an alien feature amid the Islamic architecture.

Admission to the complex was initially through the north **Puerta del Perdón Ⓐ**, but now the **Puerta de los Deanes Ⓑ** in the **Patio de los Naranjos** (Orange Tree Patio) **Ⓒ** forms the main entrance. Originally the 19 naves in the prayer hall opened directly onto the forecourt, but in Christian times the arches were bricked over to create chapels. It is no longer possible to see the minaret at the heart of the 69-m (226ft) baroque **bell tower Ⓓ**. The **Puerta de las Palmas Ⓔ** used to be the main gateway to the prayer hall.

STAGES OF DEVELOPMENT

The original **Mosque of Abd al-Rahman I**, founder of the Emirate of Córdoba, was begun in 785. The **first construction Ⓕ** was a brilliant solution for a mosque hall. Two levels of elegant arching were included in the columns which separated the 11 naves. This idea gave an extraordinary sense of height to the mosque. The arcades were doubled as the architect had columns dating from the Roman building at his disposal. The whole construction was secured by horseshoe arches linking the pillars.

In 833 **Abd al-Rahman II Ⓖ** began extending the building to the south but retained the original architectural principle. In 961 **Al-Hakam II Ⓗ** continued the enlargement in a similar way. The south wall *(kibla)* with the ★★ **prayer niche Ⓘ** *(mihrab)* was finished with exquisitely carved reliefs and coloured mosaics in Byzantine style. Above the space reserved

Puerta del Perdón Ⓐ
Ⓓ
bell tower
Ⓒ Patio de los Naranjos
Ⓑ
Puerta de los Deanes
Ⓔ Puerta de las Palmas
Mosque of Abd al-Rahman I
choir
Ⓖ Ⓝ
Capilla Mayor
Abd al-Rahman II
Capilla de Villaviciosa Ⓜ Ⓛ Capilla Real
Ⓚ final annex
Ⓙ
Puerta del Palacio Ⓗ Al-Hakam II
Ⓘ Ⓞ Capilla de Santa Teresa
prayer niche

	Abd ar-Rahman I		Al-Hakam II
	Abd ar-Rahman II		Al-Mansur

MEZQUITA

for the Caliph in front of the *mihrab* (prayer niche) were three magnificent domes. The **Puerta del Palacio** ❶ on the west wall originally linked the mosque with the ruler's palace. In 987 **Al-Mansur** ordered work to commence on the **final annex** ❶, eight additional naves to the east.

The **Capilla Real** ❶, adapted at the behest of Alfonso X as a funeral chapel, did not change the complex dramatically, nor did the first cathedral (15th century), which incorporated a domed area from the time of Al-Hakam II as an altar, the **Capilla de Villaviciosa** ❶. Only when work started on the new cathedral in 1523 involving the demolition of parts of the prayer hall did the mosque lose its uniformity.

The highlight at the heart of the cathedral is the late Baroque **choir stalls** ❶, attributed to Pedro Duque Cornejo. On the left near the prayer niche is the **Capilla de Santa Teresa** ❶ (with the treasury). Here there is a silver monstrance by Enrique de Arfe (1517).

THE JEWISH QUARTER

Outside the mosque, cross the Patio de los Naranjos and follow Calle Velázquez Bosco to **Callejón de las Flores** ❷, a picturesque alleyway noted for its floral displays. To the west lies ★★**La Judería**, formerly the Jewish quarter and a maze

Star Attractions
• Mosque's prayer niche
• La Judería

Below: Callejón de las Flores
Bottom: guided tour in the Mezquita

Map on page 39

The Zoco

On Calle Judias, the Zoco is a group of workshops clustered around a central courtyard. Here you can see craftsmen working in leather, wood and ceramic, as well as the silver for which Córdoba is justly famous. In nearby Calle Tomás Conde the Artesanía Andaluza has a good selection of Cordoban craft work.

of tiny lanes bustling with life. Cross Plaza de Juda Leví to get to Plaza Maimónides, where the **Museo Taurino** ❸ (Museum of Bullfighting; spring to autumn, Tuesday to Saturday 10am–2pm, 6–8pm, Sunday/public holidays 9.30am–3pm; admission free on Friday) is housed in a 16th-century mansion. Many of Córdoba's bullfighting heroes are celebrated here, and there is a replica of the tomb of Manoleto, perhaps the most famous of them all, who was gored to death in the ring in Linares in 1947.

Just behind the museum, Calle de los Judíos opens out on to a small plaza, where a memorial honours **Maimonides**, the distinguished medieval Jewish philosopher who was born in Córdoba in 1135.

Below: hero in the Museum of Bullfighting
Bottom: browsing in the Zoco

SURVIVING SYNAGOGUE

A few metres further on to the left you will see the plain entrance door to the ★★**Synagoga** ❹ (Tuesday to Saturday 10am–1.30pm, 3.30–5.30pm, Sunday/public holidays 10.30am–1.30pm). This small, rectangular house of prayer was built in 1314 in Mudéjar style. On the south side above the vestibule is a women's gallery. Stucco decorations on the walls form geometric designs and patterns of plants. Hebrew inscriptions quote verses from the Psalms. Córdoba's synagogue is one of three surviving medieval synagogues in Spain. The other two are in Toledo. After the Jews were expelled in 1492, the building was used as a church.

Continue along Calle de los Judíos and you will reach the ancient city gate called the **Puerta de Almodóvar** ❺, where there is a statue of the Roman philosopher Seneca (4BC–AD65) who was born in Córdoba.

If you make your way along the city wall, you will come across a monument to another famous son of Córdoba, the Arab scholar Averroës (1126–98). You will eventually reach the quiet and shady square called the **Campo de los Mártires** (Field of the Martyrs) and the ruins of a baths complex that dates from the era of the Caliphate.

THE FORTRESS

Part of the square is enclosed by the walls of the ★ **Alcázar de los Reyes Cristianos** ❻ (spring to autumn, Tuesday to Saturday 10am–2pm, 6–8pm, Sunday/public holidays 9.30am–3pm: admission free on Friday; October to April, reduced opening times), built for Alfonso XI. It was from here that the Catholic Monarchs directed military campaigns against Nasrid Granada and where, in 1486, Queen Isabela first met Christopher Columbus and agreed to back his voyage of discovery.

The palace now houses a museum of Roman artefacts. The **Patio Mudéjar** is a garden in the Moorish tradition, while the modern gardens with their fountains have much more in common with the baroque era.

Take Calle Amador de los Ríos to return to the mosque. Opposite the west side stands the 18th-century **Palacio Episcopal** ❼, built on the site of the Caliph's Palace.

Pass the triumphal column of Archangel Raphael, the patron saint of Córdoba, and the gate dating from the time of Felipe II, before reaching the famous **Puente Romano** (Roman Bridge), now a symbol of Córdoba. On the bridge is one of many images of the Archangel Raphael, with candles burning at his feet. Visible from here on the banks of the Guadalquivir are the ruins of some Moorish mills.

Star Attractions
• Synagogue

Below: Puerto de Almodóvar with Seneca's statue
Bottom: the Puente Romano

Map on page 39

STOREHOUSE OF KNOWLEDGE

At the southern end of the bridge stands the ★ **Torre de la Calahorra** ❽, a Moorish tower rebuilt during the 14th century and now home to the **Museo del Al-Andalus**, where the latest museum technology is used to bring to life the culture of old Andalusia (Monday to Sunday 10am–2pm, 4.30–8.30pm; multivision show several times a day; autumn and winter, reduced opening times).

A full appreciation of the exhibits is facilitated by headphones with commentaries in various languages. The intellectual diversity of the Moorish era (astronomy, medicine, architecture, philosophy) demonstrates just how tolerant the Jewish, Christian and Muslim cultures were and how much they influenced each other.

Below: Torre de la Calahorra detail
Bottom: enjoying the view from the tower

THREE MUSEUMS

To find the ★ **Museo Arqueológico** ❾ (Tuesday to Saturday 10am–2pm, 6–8.30pm, closed Monday; autumn and winter, reduced afternoon opening times), housed in the Palacio de Jerónimo Páez, follow Calle de la Encarnación, which starts at the north-east corner of the Mezquita. On display here are prehistoric, Roman, Visigothic and Islamic finds, most of which were discovered at Madinat al-Zahra *(see page 46)*.

The **Museo Provincial de las Bellas Artes** ❿ (spring to autumn, Wednesday to Saturday 9am–8pm, Tuesday 3–8pm, Sunday/public holidays 9am–3pm; winter, reduced opening times) is situated by **Plaza del Potro**. This museum holds an interesting collection of Andalusian baroque art and has a whole section devoted to the works of local sculptor Mateo Inurria.

In an adjoining building is the **Museo Julio Romero de Torres** (spring to autumn, Tuesday to Saturday 10am–2pm, 6–8pm, Sunday/public holidays 9.30am–3pm; free admission on Friday; winter, reduced opening times), a Cordoban 'poster' artist (1874–1930).

> **Cervantes' Inn**
> During the 16th century, Plaza del Potro was the centre of Córdoba. The square has a fountain at the centre with a statue of a colt on top (potro means colt). Posada del Potro, a former inn on the square, is of particular interest as it was mentioned in Cervantes' Don Quixote.

A Glimpse of the City's Past

Continue along Calle de San Fernando and you will come to the **Ayuntamiento** ⓫ (Town Hall) (1594–1631), near where the remains of a Roman temple have been uncovered. To the southeast lies **Plaza de la Corredera** ⓬. This rectangular square, surrounded by arcaded, four-storey houses, dates from the 17th century and once occupied an important part in Córdoba's day-to-day life, as bullfights, plays and *autos-da-fé* used to be staged here. A new market has been built, but this plaza has been in decline for many years.

Calle Hermanos López and Calle E. Redel lead up to the ★ **Palacio de Viana** ⓭ (Monday to Saturday 10am–1pm, 4–6pm, Sunday/public holidays 10am–2pm; autumn and winter, reduced opening times), a fine example of how a mansion can change over the centuries. Its rooms are clustered around no fewer than 12 patios and a garden. Take the guided tour of the grand house and gain a fascinating insight into the lifestyle of the Andalusian nobility.

Follow Calle Santa Isabel and Calle Isabel Losa and then take the steps from Calle Rincón to Plaza de los Dolores and the **Cristo de los Faroles** (Christ of the Lanterns). In the square, surrounded by eight lanterns, stands a much-revered sculpture of the crucifixion, another symbol of the city of Córdoba.

Below: colt statue on Plaza del Potro
Bottom: Christo de los Faroles

Map
on pages
80–81

Missionary Centre

The 15th-century convent of San Francisco in Palma del Río became the jumping off point for missionaries to the New World. They included Father Junipero Serra, who established California's missions, starting with San Diego in 1769. The monastery has been converted into a small hotel and restaurant where, in season, the menu features venison and boar hunted in the Sierra Morena.

Excursion to Madinat al-Zahra

Leave the city along Avenida República Argentina on the C431 in the direction of Palma de Río and after a few kilometres take the turning to ★★ **Madinat al-Zahra** (Medina Azahara) (spring and summer, Tuesday to Saturday 10am–2pm, 6–8.30pm; autumn and winter, reduced opening times).

Abd al-Rahman III chose a sheltered position for this sublime city on the southern slopes of Sierra Morena. It was intended to be the capital of the new Al-Andalus caliphate. Work started in 936 and continued for 40 years. Artisans and artists from all over the Arab world were at the disposal of experienced architects. Marble columns and capitals were shipped in from the entire Mediterranean basin. However, in 1010 Berber troops destroyed the largely self-sufficient palace complex. Later the Almoravids and Almohads plundered the site for its building materials, thus precipitating the dilapidation of the city.

Madinat al-Zahra

Restoring the Splendour

Excavations and restoration work started in 1910, exposing a city covering an area 1,500 x 750m (4,920 x 2,460ft), extending over three terraces and enclosed by a wall fortified by towers. On the highest terrace stood the palace of the caliph, Abd al-Rahman III, while on the terrace below were administrative buildings and the dwellings of senior officials.

The main reception hall, the **Salón Rico**, so-named because of its richly decorated interior, has been rebuilt to give some impression of the splendour of the original room. It is entered through a lobby with five horseshoe arches. Opposite the hall a pavilion was set in a garden surrounded by ponds.

The lower terrace was used for the servants' and soldiers' quarters, but there were also workshops, markets, public baths and, of course, the mosque. Water reached the complex via a 15-km (9-mile) aqueduct starting in the mountains.

3: Granada

Both the Moorish legacy and the topography of Granada are overwhelming. Set on three hills (Albaicín, Sacramonte and Sabika) on the lower slopes of the Sierra Nevada, the city gently merges with the *vega* below, a fertile plain cultivated by the Moors. Gleaming in the background are the snow-capped peaks of the Sierra Nevada. Nowadays it is not so easy to cast your eye over the city's backdrop as high-rise apartments dominate in the provincial capital's suburban belt. Granada's university is one of the largest in Spain.

Star Attraction
• **Madinat al-Zahra**

The Alhambra reigns supreme

HISTORY

The first of the Nasrid rulers, Mohammed ibn Jusuf ibn Nasr (1238–73), founded the kingdom of Granada in 1238, although ultimately he owed allegiance to Fernando III. Art and culture blossomed under the Nasrid dynasty. Mohammed I laid the foundation stone of the Alhambra, the only medieval Islamic palace complex in the world to have survived almost intact. However, in 1482, the Catholic monarchs, Isabela and Ferdinand, set about bringing the last Islamic enclave to an end. In 1492, after a long siege, Boabdil, the city's last Moorish king, handed over the keys of the city.

The Alhambra

The self-confidence of the Islamic rulers was marked by an awareness of the transitory nature of life. Their palaces were residences for the present, furnished in luxurious style but built from materials that they knew would not last. There were no splendid facades. In the Alhambra the patios are clustered together, linked by unassuming passageways. Behind the arcades in the fountain-adorned patios lay the private and state rooms. As well as the lavish decorations the extravagant use of water emphasised the wealth of the residents – in a land of relatively little rainfall only the rich use it purely for pleasure.

Top: surveying the city from the castle wall
Bottom: fountain in the Generalife Gardens

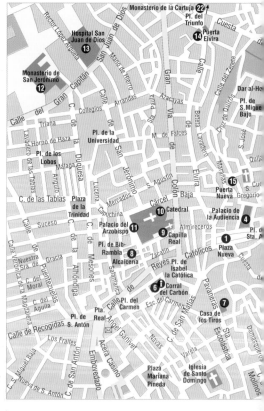

GAINING ENTRANCE

You can book admission tickets for the Alhambra with a credit card (tel: 0034/902 22 44 60), or you can buy them from any branch of the Banco Bilbao Viscaya (be careful to get the date right), or from the booking office at the Alhambra itself (if possible be there before 8am) – it is located near the new car park. It takes 20 minutes to walk from the booking office to the entrance to the palaces, but there is also a miniature railway. Once inside the Alhambra, you can stay there as long as you want. It is open from October to March, Monday to Saturday 9am–5.45pm; April to September, Monday to Saturday 8.30am–7.45pm, Sunday 9am–5pm.

Star Attraction
• **The Alhambra**

Waxing Lyrical
The beauties of the Alhambra have inspired writers and travellers throughout the centuries. In 1494, long before Washington Irving came on the scene (*see page 52*), and only two years after it had been captured by Christian forces, a German historian, Hieronymus Münzer, wrote: 'There is nothing like it in Europe; it is so magnificent, so majestic, so exquisitely fashioned... that one cannot be sure one is not in Paradise'.

ROUTE 3 GRANADA

Mirador de San Cristóbal
Alhacaba
San José **18**
Plaza Larga
Plaza Aliatar
Santa Isabel la Real **7**
ALBAICÍN
San Nicolas
Pl. del Abad
Mirador San Nicolas
Algibe
Trillo
Las Tomasas
Cjon. de los Frailes
Rosal
S. Juan de los Reyes
de los Reyes
El Bañuelo **21** **20** Casa del Castril (Museo Arqueológico)
Carrera
del Darro
Sta. Ana
San Pedro **19**
Po. del P. Manjón
← Darro
Alhambra **2**
Alcazaba
Palacios Nazari
Palacio Real de Carlos V
Puerta de las Granadas
Puerta de la Justicia
Generalife **3**
ampo del rincipe

Touring the Alhambra

Maps
on pages
48–49, 51

*Below: wall ring in the
Palacio de Carlos V
Bottom: the circular
patio of the palace*

THROUGH THE GREAT GATE

Start your explorations from **Plaza Nueva ❶** in
the centre of the city and follow the Cuesta de
Gomérez up to the Alhambra on Mount Sabika.
If you are arriving in Granada by car, take the city
motorway in the direction of the Sierra Nevada
and then follow the signs to Alhambra. The name,
meaning Red Fortress (in Arabic it's *kalat al-
Hamra*), probably derives from the reddish colour
of the outer walls.

About halfway up you will pass the Puerta de
las Granadas, embellished with the symbol of the
city (three opened pomegranates) and the coat-
of-arms of Carlos V. Just to the south of this gate
stands the Torres Bermejas, an 11th–12th-century
tower that originally formed part of the palace's
outer fortifications.

RENAISSANCE ADDITIONS

Continue through the park to the **Puerta de la
Justicia**, the Gate of Justice. This is the main
entrance to the palace complex, which is surrounded by a 2,200-m (7,215-ft) wall reinforced
with towers. Depicted above the outer gateway
arch is a hand, whose five fingers symbolise the
five pillars of Islam (profession of faith, duty of
prayer five times a day, fasting in Ramadan, the
giving of alms and duty to make a pilgrimage to
Mecca). The fortress, the oldest part of the Alhambra, can be reached via Plaza de los Aljibes on the
site of the old moat.

In 1526 Carlos V commissioned Pedro
Machuca to build a Renaissance-style palace, but
the new project resulted in the loss of part of the
Alhambra. The resulting ★ **Palacio de Carlos V**,
a square block with a circular courtyard, was
never fully completed. It currently houses the
Museo de Bellas Artes (Tuesday to Saturday
10am– 2pm).

Also installed in Carlos V's palace is the re-
opened **Museo de la Alhambra** (Tuesday to Saturday 9am–2.30pm) with a specially selected
collection reflecting Islamic art in Spain. It is def-
initely worth a visit, and it is free.

MYRTLE AND GOLD

Cross the Jardines de Machuca to reach the ★★★**Alhambra Palace ❷**. The **Mexuar ❹**, the first room, was an audience chamber for the Nasrid princes, the place where justice was dispensed. After the *reconquista* it was converted into a chapel. The adjoining **Patio del Mexuar ❸** leads to the palace's main section. Located to the north is the **Cuarto Dorado ❺**, the Golden Room, which owes its name to the gold patterns on the *artesonado* ceiling. This dates from the time of the Catholic Monarchs.

The adjoining ★★**Patio de Arrayanes** (Myrtle Patio) ❹ is one of two wings that have survived more or less unscathed. In the time of Jusuf I (1333–54) it was the architectural centrepiece of the palace complex and the heart of courtly life. The dominant feature is the long, narrow pool surrounded by clipped myrtle hedges.

HIGHLIGHTS OF THE PALACE

To the north stands the **Torre de Comares**, plain from the outside but masking a magnificent interior. Enter the tower through the narrow anteroom known as the **Sala de Barca ❹**, before stepping into the ★★**Salón de los Embajadores ❹**, the Ambassadors' Hall. A cedar-wood dome with inlaid stars, made from 8,000 pieces – which rep-

Star Attractions
•**Patio de Arrayanes**
•**Salón de los Embajadores**

Patio de Arrayanes

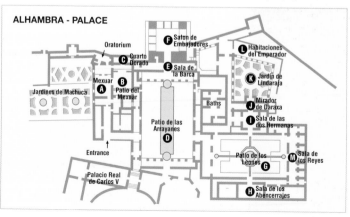

Maps on pages 48–49, 51

👁 Alhambra at night

A tour of the Alhambra at night when the palace rooms are floodlit, highlighting the three-dimensional splendour of the stucco decor, can be a memorable experience.

Tours run from April to September, Tuesday, Thursday and Saturday 10–11.45pm; October to March, Saturday 8–9.45pm. Admission tickets are available 15 minutes or so earlier in the small building next to the Puerta del Vino opposite the Palace of Carlos V. Take a taxi home (tel: 958 28 06 54), as it is not advisable to walk the streets around the Alhambra at night.

Patio de los Leones

resent the seven heavens of Islam – gives this magnificent chamber a sense of great height. The walls above a plinth made from colourful glazed tiles are decorated with splendid filigree arabesques. In the niche opposite the entrance stood the throne of the Nasrid kings, placed here so that the ruler could study his visitors while keeping his own face hidden in the shade.

The ★ ★ ★ **Patio de los Leones** Ⓖ (Lion Patio), built under Mohammed V (1354–91), is the second unscathed wing of the palace. The galleries running round it were then a totally new element in Islamic architecture, inspired by Christian cloisters. In the centre, where the paths meet, is the fountain, borne by twelve lions. Chiselled into the fountain wall is an inscription that acclaims the architectural perfection of the Alhambra just as much as the power of the ruler.

DOMES, BATHS AND GARDENS

Just off the Lion Patio lies the ★ **Sala de los Abencerrajes** Ⓗ with a beautiful star-shaped stalactite dome. Opposite is the ★★ **Sala de las Dos Hermanas** Ⓘ, the Hall of the Two Sisters, which also has an exquisite dome; the name refers to two enormous marble slabs in its floor.

Tagged on to the northern transverse section is a small room, the **Mirador de Daraxa** Ⓙ, which overlooks the **Jardín de Lindaraja** Ⓚ. In the **Habitaciones del Emperador** Ⓛ (Emperor Carlos V's Rooms), which surround this garden, is a plaque dedicated to the American writer, Washington Irving, who spent some months here in 1829, and helped put Granada on the map.

Linked to the narrow, eastern side of the Patio de los Leones is the **Sala de los Reyes** Ⓜ, the Kings' Hall. Its alcoves have ceiling paintings on leather depicting scenes from courtly life.

The Patio de los Leones opens on to the **Jardín de Lindaraja**. After crossing the chambers built for Carlos V, you will come to the **Moorish baths**. The tour ends at the **Jardines del Partal** where a pavilion, the only remaining part of an old palace, stands in the gardens.

GENERALIFE GARDENS

Leaving via the Jardines del Partal, you take the path beside the 16th-century Santa María de la Alhambra church and past the old Franciscan monastery, now the **Parador de San Francisco**, one of the best-sited of all the Spanish paradors.

This path leads you to the ★★ **Generalife ❸** palace and gardens, which were once the summer residence for the sultans. The gardens are unforgettable, the most magnificent in Spain. Designed in the 13th century they have undergone many changes, but the numerous pools, fountains and water jets, the most Arabic of the remaining features, mean that the cooling sound of water is never far away. The lovely **Escalera de Agua** is exactly what its Spanish name says – a staircase of flowing water.

On the way back to town you could take a quick look at the **Museo Manuel de Falla** (Tuesday to Saturday 10am–3pm) in Calle Antequerela Alta, if you are interested in music. Carry on through the Judería to **Campo del Príncipe**, where there are lots of of inviting places to eat.

THE OLD CITY

The Alhambra and Generalife are the reason most people come here, but Granada has much more to offer and the Old City is well worth exploring.

Star Attractions
• **Patio de los Leones**
• **Sala de las Dos Hermanas**
• **Generalife**

Below: Generalife Gardens
Bottom: the gardens and Alhambra walls

Map
on pages
48–49

*Below in the heart
of the Alcaicería
Bottom: refreshments
in the Old Town*

Beside the central **Plaza Nueva** stand the **Palacio de la Audiencia** ❹, the province's high court, and the delightful little Mudéjar **Santa Ana** ❺ church with a plateresque west portal. Follow Calle de los Reyes Católicos towards the city centre and the **Corral del Carbón** ❻, the Nasrid caravanserai (April to September, Monday to Saturday 9am–1pm, 4–7pm; October to March, Monday to Saturday 9am–8pm, Sunday 10am–2pm). Now fully restored, it is occupied by a tourist information office and a municipal gallery often used as a venue for temporary exhibitions. During the summer, open-air performances are staged in the courtyard.

In Calle de Pavaneras you will find the 16th-century **Casa de los Tiros** ❼. The small statues on the otherwise plain facade represent Hercules, Theseus, Jason, Hector and Mercury. This privately owned mansion houses a museum on the history of Granada (temporarily closed).

ROYAL CHAPEL

Return through the tiny lanes, crossing Calle de los Reyes Católicos and past the **Alcaicería** ❽, once the silk market, but now mainly souvenir shops. Although it was destroyed by fire in 1843, the quarter has been rebuilt in its original style and still radiates the charm of an oriental souk.

The ★★ **Capilla Real** ❾ (Royal Chapel; daily 10.30am–1pm, 4–7pm, Sunday/public holidays 11am–1pm) was built between 1504 and 1521 as a mausoleum for Ferdinand and Isabela, the Catholic Monarchs, who unified Spain. It stands on Calle de los Oficios (entrance through the old stock exchange). Marble monuments represent Ferdinand and Isabela, their daughter Juana la Loca (the Mad) and Felipe el Hermoso (the Handsome). The carved altar wall is dedicated to John the Baptist and John the Evangelist, and there is a splendid altar grille.

THE CATHEDRAL

The neighbouring ★★ **Catedral** ❿ (hours as for the Capilla Real; entrance on Gran Vía) was built in 1523 on the site of the city's main mosque to commemorate the victory of the Catholic Monarchs. It consists of five naves with side chapels and an unusual circular chancel with a gallery. The west facade was added in 1669 in the form of a huge triumphal arch. Like many other features in the church, it is the work of the Granadian master, Alonso Cano, who is buried in the precincts. One of Cano's masterpieces, the small carved figure of María Immaculata, can be seen in the sacristy.

To explore the area around the cathedral start at the square by the west facade, pass the **Palacio del Arzobispo** ⓫ and finish at the bustling **Plaza Bib-Rambla**, where there is a lively atmosphere among the flower stalls, pavement cafes and kiosks.

SAN JERONIMO

On the other side of the Cathedral, Calle de San Jerónimo heads north across Plaza de la Universidad to the **Monasterio de San Jerónimo** ⓬, founded by royal edict in 1492. Buried in the church is Don Gonzalo Fernández de Córdoba (d. 1515), popularly known as El Gran Capitán, the commander of the Catholic Monarchs' troops. The monastery has two 16th-century cloisters.

Star Attractions
• Capilla Real
• Catedral

Below: Hercules statue on Casa de los Tiros
Bottom: inside the Catedral

Map on pages 48–49

Sacramonte

Sacramonte, the Holy Hill to the north of the Albaicín, used to be one of the best-known parts of Granada. The caves that riddled the hillsides were the homes of gypsies and you used to be able to see genuine flamenco there. Now the gypsies have been rehoused, and their community broken up. There are still a few flamenco shows in Sacramonte, but they are strictly for tourists.

Hospital San Juan de Díos

Situated close by is the baroque **Hospital San Juan de Díos** ⑬. From Calle San Juan de Díos cross Avenida de la Constitución to reach the **Jardines del Triunfo** gardens.

Making your way back to the city centre along Paseo del Triunfo, you will pass the Moorish **Puerta Elvira** ⑭ town gate, which dates from the 11th century. It was through this gate that the Catholic Monarchs entered Granada in 1492.

ALBAICIN

The white ★★ **Albaicín** quarter of winding alleyways and narrow staircases clings to the hill across from the Alhambra. This district with its *carmenes* (country houses with gardens) is now under a protection order. A terrace near San Nicolás church in the heart of the quarter provides a magnificent **panoramic view** of the Alhambra.

A little further on as you climb the hill is the **Puerta Nueva** ⑮, once a Zirid fortress (11th century). Two footpaths lead from here down to the Río Darro. To the west, on Callejón de las Monjas, stands the Nasrid palace, **Dar al-Horra** ⑯ (Monday only, 10am–1pm by appointment; tel: 958 22 14 37), although little remains apart from a small patio with pools and the surrounding alcoves. It now belongs to the **Santa Isabel la Real** monastery ⑰, which was founded in 1501 by Queen Isabela. Part of the palace was demolished to make way for the monastery. Calle San José leads to **San José** ⑱, the Mudéjar church whose bell tower was originally the minaret of an Almoravid mosque. Proceed downhill and you will come to Plaza Nueva.

SAN PEDRO

Head eastwards from the busy Plaza Larga at the heart of the Albaicín quarter and you will find the church of San Salvador. From here cut through the narrow Calle Tomasas and Calle San Agustín to Cuesta del Chapiz and then descend between the thick white walls to Paseo Padre Manjón and its **terraced cafes** beside the Río Darro.

Downstream on the left stands the church of **San Pedro ⓳**, noted for its fine *artesonado* ceiling. **Casa del Castril ⓴**, the Renaissance palace opposite, dates from 1539 and is now the **Museo Arqueológico** (Tuesday to Thursday 3–8pm, Wednesday to Saturday 9am–8pm, Sunday 9am–2.30pm). The collection includes prehistoric, Roman and Visigothic finds and art and artefacts from Moorish times.

A little further on is **El Bañuelo ㉑** (Tuesday to Saturday 10am–2pm), a well-preserved Arab baths complex dating from the 11th century. The marble floor in the main room is original; some of the capitals date from Visigoth and Umayyad times. The entrance is through a lovely shady patio, where the air is filled with birdsong.

EL CAPITAN'S MONASTERY

The grand **Monasterio de la Cartuja ㉒** (April to September, daily 10am–1pm, 4–8pm, Sunday 10am–noon; October to March, until 6pm) is in the northern outskirts of the city (follow signs to La Cartuja). It was founded in 1506 by El Gran Capitán, the man who ran the Catholic Monarchs' military campaigns. The cloisters and church are Renaissance, the sacristy, a perfect example of Churrigueresque style, and the opulent baroque **Sagrario**, were added during the 18th century.

Star Attraction
• The Albaicín

Below: Iglesia de Santa Ana on Plaza Nueva
Bottom: Carrera del Darro in the Albaicín

Map on pages 58–59

4: Spain's Sunshine Coast

Almería – Salobreña – Málaga – Torremolinos – Benalmádena – Fuengirola – Marbella – Estepona

Below: sign to the sights in Almería
Bottom: Almería local

This tour along the Costa del Sol includes the cities of Almería and Málaga, and then hugs the coast with stops in Torremolinos, Fuengirola, Marbella and San Pedro de Alcántara, ending in Estepona. We also take a detour into the impressive hinterland. There is plenty to explore in the towns, which are far more than staging posts for international travellers on their way to the sun. Allow for a least one overnight stop. Bus services along the Costa del Sol are very good, although private transport is preferable.

ALMERIA

The town of ★ **Almería** (pop. 170,000) lies in a broad bay overlooked by mountains. This part of Andalusia is one of the driest regions on the Iberian peninsula – indeed the whole of Europe. Almería's harbour is one of the busiest on the Spanish Mediterranean coast. Exports include iron ore from the mines in the Sierra de los Filabres and agricultural produce from the Andarax basin and the other valleys along the coastal strip, where early fruit crops are grown under polythene. Thanks to its hot, dry climate in summer and very mild winters – some 3,000

hours of sunshine a year – Almería has become an important centre for solar energy technology as well as a major tourist centre.

Towering over the Old Town are the ruins of the **★★ Alcazaba**, which can be reached on foot from Plaza de la Constitución (daily 9am–1.30pm, 3.30–7.30pm). This imposing fortification consisting of three battlemented compounds was begun under Abd ar-Rahman III, the first caliph of Córdoba. The last major additions date from the time of the Catholic Monarchs. Excavation work in the second compound has exposed the ground plan of the former palace. The **Torre del Homanaje** (15th century) and the upper area has largely survived the ravages of time. A defensive wall links the Alcazaba site with the **Castillo de San Cristóbal** on the neighbouring hill.

THE CATHEDRAL TO THE HARBOUR

Almería's **Catedral** (Monday to Friday 10am–5pm, Saturday 10am–1pm) is sited close to the Plaza de la Constitución. Work started on the church in 1524, on the site of a mosque destroyed in an earthquake two years earlier. During the 16th century the town was under constant threat from Turkish and Berber pirates, which explains why the main body of the cathedral is fortified with four towers. The severe overall impression is lightened somewhat by Renaissance portals.

The most impressive feature of the triple-nave interior is an array of carved choir stalls (1560) by Juan de Orea.

You can reach the harbour from the rear of the cathedral. If you take the Nicolás Salmerón seaside promenade towards the east, you will come to

Star Attraction
• Almería's Alcazaba

Below: steps to the Alcazaba
Bottom: the wall to Castillo de San Cristóbal

ROUTE 4

0   20 km

Map on pages 58–59

Avenida de Federico García Lorca, which serves as the boundary between the old and new town.

In the **Museo de Bellas Artes** (Monday to Friday 10am–2pm, 4–6pm), near the railway station, you will find Phoenician and Roman exhibits, given a home here after the closure of the Archaeological Museum, whose future is in doubt.

The overall impression of Almería is anything but uniform. The Chanca gypsy quarter between the Old Town and the Alcazaba, the old-fashioned shopping lanes, the modern facades in Paseo de Almería and the harbour combine to form an diverse and interesting cityscape.

Mini-Hollywood

The Sierra de Alhamilla, situated 24km (15 miles) to the northeast of Almería, is so dry and inhospitable that it could easily be mistaken for Arizona, and some film producers have sought to re-create the Wild West here. Many people will recognise the backdrop from the Italian 'Spaghetti Westerns' directed by Sergio Leone, or from *Lawrence of Arabia*.

The full-scale, Western stage set at **Mini-Hollywood** (by the N340) welcomes visitors, who can enjoy live cowboy performances (daily noon and 5pm; mid-June to mid-September, also at 8pm).

COASTAL HIGHLIGHTS

West of Almería the coast has a backdrop of plastic-clad hillsides, where fruit and vegetables grow all year round. The road passes through the busy commercial centre of El Ejido, before reaching ★ **Salobreña**, 117km (73 miles) from Almería. It stands high on a rock in the middle of a semi-circular coastal strip, an ochre-coloured castle crowning the summit with white houses clustered at its feet. Fields of sugar cane – the molasses is used to make rum – surround the village. The main crop in the next valley, near **Almuñécar**, is the sweet *cherimoya* (custard apple).

El Peñon restaurant in Salobreña

NERJA

The next place worth a stop is ★ **Nerja**, an attractive holiday resort, situated between two bays, that has not been spoilt by tower blocks. Outside the village are the impressive ★ **Cuevas de Nerja** (daily 10am–2pm, 4–6.30pm; July/August until 8pm; tel: 952 52 95 20), with strange stalactite formations and faded wall paintings. In August the caves become a venue for concerts and dance performances.

DETOUR TO ALHAMA DE GRANADA

The next section of this route is characterised by an impressive juxtaposition of coastline and sheer mountains. At the high-rise settlement of **Torre del Mar** turn inland along the C355 and continue for 4km (2½ miles) as far as **Vélez Málaga** (pop. 53,000), which has an attractive Old Town. At the highest point stand the watchtowers of a Moorish fortress. A short distance away is the 16th-century church of Santa María with some superb examples of Mudéjar architecture.

Continue uphill beside the river to the Puerto de Zafarraya pass. Situated at (920m/3,018ft), it provides a panoramic view of the highest peaks in the **Sierra de Almijara**, which reach a height of 1,832m (6,010ft).

Heading inland, about halfway between Vélez Málaga and Granada, at an altitude of 883m (2,897ft), lies **Alhama de Granada** (pop. 6,000), formerly a stopping point for trading caravans. As far back as Moorish times this picturesque little town was appreciated for its thermal springs, said to be beneficial to rheumatism sufferers.

Below: painted tile in Nerja
Bottom: Málaga surveyed from the Gibralfaro

MALAGA

Some 30km (18 miles) from Vélez Málaga, the provincial capital of ★ **Málaga** (pop. 532,000) lies at the foot of the Montes de Málaga in the largest lowland plain along this section of coast. Cotton, sugar cane, citrus fruits, figs and grapes are cultivated here. Outsiders often say that the city

Map on page 63

of Málaga has 'overflowed'. Dispersed around a bustling, in places elegant, city centre with a parkland promenade, a traditional harbour and a bizarre, unfinished cathedral, are sprawling estates of holiday apartments and depressing residential areas.

EXPLORING THE PAST

Towering above the eastern side of the city is **Gibralfaro** or 'lighthouse mountain' (follow signs to the *parador*). Because of its strategic importance, this hill has always been crowned by some form of fortification. The ruins of the **Castillo del Gibralfaro** ❶ date from Nasrid times, but only the restored walls remain. At the foot of the citadel lies the ★ **Alcazaba** ❷, a palace that is linked to the Castillo by a parapet. To enter the Alcazaba, which is surrounded by a double ring of walls, you must negotiate a narrow, winding passage; some of the masonry you will pass is of Roman origin. Immediately outside the entrance on the left you will see the **Teatro Romano** (1st century AD) on a hillside.

Below: Málaga's Teatro Romano
Bottom: sculpture in the Casa Natal de Picasso

The Alcazaba was the residence of the Moorish ruler of Málaga. Some sections of it date back to Umayyad times but the site was rebuilt by the Nasrids and comes across as a plainer version of the Alhambra in Granada. It now houses the **Museo Arqueológico** (Monday, Wednesday to Sunday 9.30am–6.30pm), displaying Roman sculptures, Moorish pottery, carved beams and decorated marble slabs.

ON PICASSO'S TRAIL

You can skirt round the hill from the Gibralfaro on Calle Ferrándiz and then take Calle de la Victoria to **Plaza del Merced**. Here, at No. 15, is the houses where Pablo Picasso was born in 1881, the ★ **Casa Natal de Picasso** ❸ (Monday to Saturday 10am–2pm, 5–8pm, Sunday 11am–2pm). It is the headquarters of the Picasso Foundation and contains many of his works, donated by his daughter-in-law, who inspired the foundation.

Calle del Císter runs from the Alcazaba to the single-towered ★★ **Catedral** ❹ (Monday to Saturday 10am–6.45pm). Although the foundations were laid in 1528, building work continued for over 200 years. The interior is an impressive triple-nave, 48m (157ft) high. The figures of saints on the magnificent 17th-century choir stalls, some by Alonso Cano and Pedro de Mena, are among the highlights of Spanish woodcarving. The oldest piece is the late-Gothic *retablo* for the Capilla de Santa Bárbara in the ambulatory.

By the square in front of the west facade stands the **Palacio Episcopal** housing the Diocesan Museum (temporarily closed). Take Calle de San Agustín over to the Renaissance **Palacio de los Condes de Buenavista**, a building that has Moorish origins. Currently undergoing renovation, it is due to open in 2002 as the **Museo Picasso**. It used to house the **Museo Provincial de Bellas Artes**, but this is now closed and will shortly move to a new home. The old Convento de Trinidad is the Malagueños preferred site.

If you turn to the right from here into Calle Alamos, you will alight on **Taberna Pimpi**, a bar where excellent sherry and delicious cheese and ham *tapas* are served.

Star Attraction
• **Málaga's Catedral**

The Palacio Episcopal

Maps
on pages
58–59, 63

Benalmádena

One of Andalusia's famous white villages, Benalmádena, lies a few kilometres inland, about half way between Torremolinos and Fuengirola, some 350m (1,150 ft) above sea level. Its bright houses are ablaze with flowers and orange trees shade its two plazas. It is surprisingly uncrowded and has a small **Museo d'Arte Precolombiano** (Mon–Fri 10am–2pm, 4–6pm).

Below: tiled bench along the Paseo del Parque
Bottom: Málaga's bullring

SMALL DIVERSIONS

A popular place for an evening stroll – the customary *paseo* – is the late 19th-century **Paseo del Parque**, which extends from Plaza de la Marina to the **bullring**, with gardens, open-air cafes, children's playgrounds and a number of kiosks.

The **Mercado Central** near Alameda Principal is an attractive building designed in neo-Mudéjar style. A vast array of fruit, vegetables, dried fruit, saffron and other spices, cooked meats and cheeses are on sale in the market.

WEST OF MALAGA

The A7/E15 coast road leaves Málaga to the southwest, passing through the best-known section of the Costa del Sol, the centrepiece of Spanish tourism. This conurbation has one of the highest population densities in Spain. If you want to make a detour into the hinterland, take the N321 from Málaga to Antequera *(see page 85)* via the Puerto de las Pedrizas pass (780m/2,560ft).

THE ROAD TO MARBELLA

In recent decades, holiday developments have sprung up along the full length of this coastal strip, taking advantage of the wonderful beaches. Many of them have copied Moorish architectural styles, the lines interspersed with gardens and parkland.

Only 8km (5 miles) from Málaga lies **Torremolinos**, the resort that is synonymous with the package-holiday aspect of the Costa. Once a pretty little town, it is now wall-to-wall bars and discos, with a tourist population that outnumbers the locals by about four to one.

The highway next takes you to **Fuengirola**, a popular resort with a good beach and an attractive, pedestrianised old town, but far too many high-rise apartment blocks.

Some 65km (40 miles) west of Málaga, you reach ★★ **Marbella** (pop. 87,000), the oldest and most exclusive holiday resort on the Costa del Sol, with miles of white, sandy beaches. Marbella easily outdoes its rivals in elegance, and has an ambience that comes from being a genuine, old town, not just a tourist development.

At the heart of the delightful town centre is **Plaza de los Naranjos** with its orange trees and decorative lighting, a bronze bust of King Juan Carlos and an octagonal marble fountain. The **Ayuntamiento** (Town Hall), built between the 16th and 18th century, also overlooks this square.

The flower-bedecked Calle del Carmen leads to the **Iglesia de la Encarnación** (16th century). Numerous small restaurants, cafes and boutiques occupy the whitewashed buildings that line the attractive, narrow lanes.

Since the 1960s Marbella has been associated with luxury and the super-rich. **Puerto Banús**, an exclusive marina 6km (4 miles) to the west of town, is the place to watch the jet set going about their gilded lives.

AUTHENTIC ESTEPONA

About 2km (1 mile) inland lies **San Pedro de Alcántara**, a little town colonised by English and American expats when Marbella began to expand.

The last port of call is ★ **Estepona**, 16 km (10 miles) away, the most Spanish of the resorts. Beside its beautiful beaches runs an elegant promenade and narrow lanes with whitewashed houses surround the pretty **Plaza de las Flores**.

Star Attraction
• Marbella

Below: Iglesia de la Encarnación in Marbella
Bottom: the beach at Puerto Banús

Map on page 66

Pillars of Hercules, Gibraltar

5: Mediterranean to Atlantic

Gibraltar – Algeciras – Tarifa – Vejer de la Frontera – Cádiz – Sanlúcar de Barrameda

Starting from Gibraltar, the British enclave to the east of the Straits of Gibraltar, this route follows the southern coast to Cádiz. As well as acquainting yourself with the beautiful and often deserted sandy beaches that border the Atlantic Ocean, you will also discover two of the famous 'white villages' of Andalusia. Allow at least two days for this route as you will want plenty of time to explore Cádiz and to stop off for an occasional dip in the sea.

GIBRALTAR

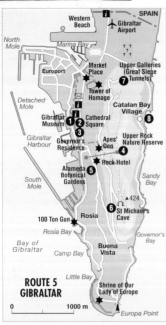

Following the N340 from the north, at San Roque the road forks off to ★★ **Gibraltar**. In antiquity the famous rock here was known as Calpe, but was later named Djebel al-Tariq (Tariq's Mountain) after the Berber governor of Tangier. In time this became corrupted to Gibraltar. Tarik ibn Ziyad had intended only to make a reconnaissance trip from Africa, but his victory over the Visigoths at the battle of Jerez de la Frontera in July 711 culminated in his conquest of the whole peninsula. Spanish armies recaptured Gibraltar in 1309 but were unable to hold it, and the reconquest did not take place until 1462.

It was in 1704, during the War of the Spanish Succession, that British forces took the Rock (as it is known) and in the Treaty of Utrecht (1713) Spain was forced to cede it to Britain 'in perpetuity'. In 1967 a referendum showed that the people wanted to remain under British rule, but in 1969 General Franco cut off land links with Gibraltar and until 1985 it could only be reached by sea. Relations are more cordial now but, understandably, the whole question of sovereignty remains a contentious issue.

ROUTE 5
GIBRALTAR

0   1000 m

UNMISTAKABLY ENGLISH

The best way to enter Gibraltar nowadays is on foot. Border controls make it absolutely clear that this piece of land is under British sovereignty – even given the commanding position of the **Moor's Castle**, which has survived from Muslim times, over the rock. English architecture in the form of the cathedral, **St Mary the Crowned** (19th century) or the seat of the governor in **Main Street**, predominates. Even the post boxes are bright red and the policemen's uniforms are unmistakably English. Duty-free shops and British pubs – selling English beer, naturally – line the attractively renovated Main Street

The ★★ **Gibraltar Museum ❶** (Monday to Friday 10am–6pm, Saturday 10am–2pm) is dedicated to the history of the Rock and more specifically to Admiral Lord Nelson, who died in the Battle of Trafalgar in 1805. His ship, the *Victory*, was towed back to Gibraltar, with his body preserved in a cask of brandy. The museum is connected by tunnels to the 14th-century **Moorish Baths**. Nearby, the **Trafalgar Cemetery** holds the remains of British seamen who died at Trafalgar and in several other naval battles during the 18th and early 19th century.

Close to the museum is **Cathedral Square ❷**, notable for the row of nine cannons that face out into the bay.

Star Attraction
• **Gibraltar and its Rock**

Top: street furniture
Middle: local architecture
Bottom: the Rock of Gibraltar

Maps on pages 66 & 69

Monkey Business

The famous tailless monkeys – Barbary apes – of Gibraltar were probably brought by the Moors, as a similar species exists in the Atlas Mountains, but there is a story that they made their way across the Straits through underground tunnels. According to legend, Gibraltar will only return to Spanish rule when the last monkey leaves the Rock. When numbers were low, during World War II, Winston Churchill put the army in charge and the Apes' Den was built (daily 9.30am–7pm).

Monkey business on the Rock

The **Governor's Residence** ❸ on Main Street is housed in a former Franciscan monastery, built in 1531. The weekday ceremony of the changing of the guards always attracts visitors.

Take a cable car ride to the ★ **Upper Rock Nature Reserve** ❹ on the western side of the Rock (daily every 15 minutes 9.30am–5pm; ticket includes admission to the Ape's Den and St Michael's Cave). The cable car station is close to the attractive **Alameda Botanical Gardens** ❺ and nearby is the famous Rock Hotel, with marvelous views, along with a small casino.

★ **St Michael's Cave** ❻ (daily 9.30am–7pm), a short walk from the Apes' Den *(see box)* is a vast cavern with dramatic, illuminated stalactites. Legend has it that this cave is bottomless. At the northwest end of the Rock is the entrance to the **Upper Galleries** ❼ (daily 9.30am–7pm), also known as the **Great Siege Tunnels**, for it was from here that the Brirtish repulsed the Spanish fleet. If you feel in need of a swim after this, head to **Catalan Bay** ❽, Gibraltar's best beach.

ALGECIRAS

★ **Algeciras** (pop. 104,000; 20km/12 miles from Gibraltar) is a major fishing port and also a ferry terminal for traffic to and from Morocco (2–3 ferries daily). It's atmospheric, if not particularly attractive. The bustling atmosphere emanates from the port area with **Avenida la Marina** the focal point for travellers. This is where you will find travel agencies selling tickets for the 2-hour crossing to Morocco. It is fun to watch events unfold outside the run-down hotels and pavement cafes, but do take care of your belongings.

The **Plaza Alta** above the harbour has wonderful views, tiled benches illustrating the adventures of Don Quixote, a baroque church, **Nuestra Señora de la Palma**, and a good wine bar.

On clear days the view extends as far as the Moroccan Rif Mountains. The so-called **Pillars of Hercules** can be spotted on both sides of the Straits. On the African side is **Mount Hacho**, on the European side, **Gibraltar**. According to

Greek mythology, Hercules pushed the two rocks apart to open the way from the Mediterranean into the Atlantic Ocean.

Star Attraction
•**Tarifa and its beaches**

TARIFA

★★ **Tarifa** (17km/10 miles from Algeciras) is named after the Berber warrior, Tarif ibn Malik. He landed here with his army in 710 on a sortie to test the waters for a full-scale assault the following year. At first glance Tarifa, with its white houses and almost constant sand-bearing wind, looks almost African. At the heart of the town, sheltered by the remains of a wall built in Moorish times, traces of the original settlement can still be seen.

Old Town alley in Tarifa

The Moorish **Alcázar** (10th–13th century) with its numerous battlements rises up above the town. The most interesting part is the octagonal **Torre de Guzmán el Bueno**, named after Alfonso Pérez Guzmán, the commander who heroically led the defence of the town against the Moors in 1294 and whose descendant and namesake was later to

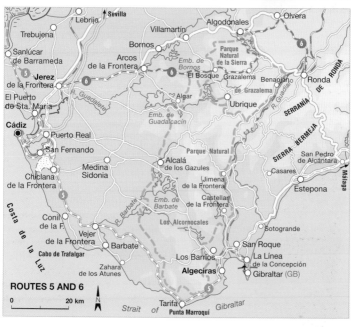

ROUTES 5 AND 6

0   20 km

Map on page 69

lead the Armada against the English. Next to the Alcázar lies the attractive **Plaza de Santa María**, from where you can gain access to the **mirador** (viewing platform). On the skyline to the south you should be able to pick out the jagged, grey silhouette of the Moroccan Rif Mountains, which at night glimmer with thousands of tiny lights.

Because of its strategically important position, Tarifa has always been coveted by the military. In the 18th century, a new fortress was built on the **Isla de las Palomas** (Dove Island; closed to the public). If you stand on the causeway that connects it with the town, the Atlantic Ocean will be on one side, the Mediterranean on the other.

Tarifa is now a top venue for windsurfers from all over Europe and consequently has lots of windsurfng schools as well as cafes and bars catering for an energetic young crowd.

The southernmost point of Europe, **Punta Marroquí**, is not far away. From here, it is only 13km (8 miles) across the Straits to Africa.

Below: view to Morocco across the Strait
Bottom: unspoilt coast

A TYPICAL 'WHITE VILLAGE'

The road now turns inland, crossing a hilly landscape. Since 1992 wind turbines have been generating electricity from the constant, buffeting wind. At intervals along what is known as the **Costa de la Luz**, a still largely unspoilt section of coast, are campsites and small hotel complexes.

Set on a steep mountain ridge above the Río Barbate, where the Muslims defeated the Visigoths in 711, is the typical *pueblo blanco* (white village) of ★ **Vejer de la Frontera**. Narrow alleys wind between white houses built around cool patios up to the ruins of the Moorish *castillo*. During the Middle Ages, the Jewish quarter (still well preserved) extended along the town wall by the Paseo de las Cobijadas. The church of **El Salvador** reveals elements of Mudéjar style.

MEDINA SIDONIA

If you have time, it is worth making a detour (22km/13 miles) from Vejer de la Frontera along the C343 to **Medina Sidonia**, which perches on the crest of a hill. It is named after the noble Medina Sidonia family, one of whom, another Alfonso Pérez Guzmán, led the Spanish Armada against the English in 1588.

Enter the tiny Old Town through the Moorish **Arco de la Pastora**. A little further on stands an Augustinian convent (17th century). If you enquire at the gate it is usually possible to view the convent church. A path runs from Santa María la Coronada to the ruins of the castle, from where there is a magnificent view over the surrounding countryside. If you want to stop for refreshments, there are two cafes in the rectangular plaza.

CADIZ

Returning to the main route, as you approach Cádiz you will round the **Bahía de Cádiz** with its salt-beds bordered by settlements. Dockyards and fisheries have merged together to create a vast, industrial zone.

★★**Cádiz** (pop. 154,000) some 90km (56 miles) from Tarifa, is probably the oldest town in Spain. The Phoenicians founded their first trading post on the Iberian peninsula here – known as Gadir – around 1,000BC. As a port and centre for trade it was often targeted by pirates. During the Middle Ages, it was attacked by the

Star Attraction
• **Cádiz**

Below: church tower in Medina Sidonia
Bottom: the Catedral Nueva in Cádiz

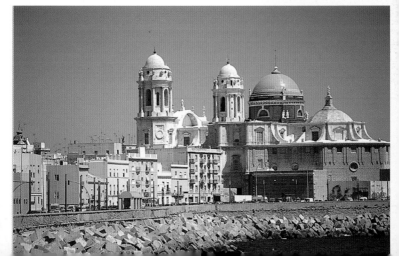

Map
on page
72

Beard-singeing

In 1587, English privateer Sir Francis Drake attacked the Spanish Armada as it lay at anchor in the Bay of Cádiz. Seizing some ships and burning others he then razed the town before rampaging up and down the coast. His laconic comment, history records, was that he had 'singed the beard of the King of Spain'.

Normans, and in the 16th century by the English fleet under Sir Francis Drake *(see box)*. After the conquest of the Americas, Cádiz served as a base and place of refuge for the Spanish fleet. Every autumn a convoy of ships sailed westward on the trade winds for Havana. After the port at Seville had silted up, Cádiz took over the virtual monopoly on the Spanish-American trade in gold and silver; it remained the wealthiest port in Spain until 1778.

During the Spanish War of Independence, Napoleonic troops failed to take the port and in 1812 deputies from the National Assembly *(Cortes)* proclaimed the Constitution of Cádiz in the San Felipe Neri church – a groundbreaking event as it was the blueprint for a liberal Spain under a constitutional monarchy. The city's status as capital of free Spain only lasted until 1814.

Cádiz is now famous for its *Carnaval*, a huge two-week-long Shrovetide festival. It's one of the biggest in Spain, especially well known for the satirical songs composed and sung by wandering bands of brightly-costumed musicians.

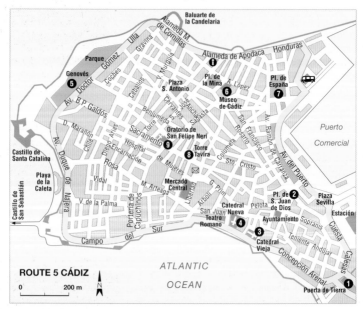

ROUTE 5 CÁDIZ
0   200 m
ATLANTIC OCEAN

A CITY OF TWO HALVES

This lively city can be split into two discrete halves: the Old Town squashed into the end of a 9-km (5-mile) long peninsula and the modern city that has grown up away from the sea. Enter the Old Town through the **Puerta de Tierra ❶**, part of the town's fortifications (17/18th century).

The road to the right leads to the main square, **Plaza de San Juan de Dios ❷**, while on the left is the coastal promenade. Right from the start Cádiz comes across as an unusual town. A salty white sheen covers the houses, its baroque church architecture sitting uneasily with the shabby harbour quarter. You will soon find yourself outside the **Catedral Vieja ❸**, dating from 1262. Now known as the **Iglesia de Santa Cruz**, it was rebuilt during the 17th century after its destruction at the hands of the Earl of Essex in 1596.

Work on the **Catedral Nueva ❹**, the last of the great Andalusian cathedrals, began in 1722 (Tuesday to Saturday 10am–1pm). The striking 'gilded' dome above the crossing looks impressive from afar, but is in fact made from glazed yellow tiles. The architects clearly looked towards the cathedrals in Granada and Málaga for their inspiration, but abandoned the severity of the Renaissance buildings in favour of a lighter touch. The nave is broken up by a huge choir with wonderful ★ **choir stalls** by Agustín de Perea (18th century). The treasury holds several precious pieces of silverware, including a monstrance by Enrique de Arfe.

COVERING THE WATERFRONT

Following the waterfront, you will come to the **Castillo de Santa Catalina** and the **Parque de Genovés ❺**, and a little further on, **Plaza de Mina**, a beautiful shady square frequented by young people in the evening. There's a good range of *tapas* bars and cafes nearby.

Beside the plaza is the city's municipal museum, the **Museo de Cádiz ❻** (Tuesday 2.30–8pm, Wednesday to Saturday 9am–8pm, Sunday 9.30am–2.30pm). As well as archaeological finds relating to the history of Cádiz, it has

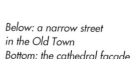

Star Attraction
• **Cádiz Old Town and Cathedral**

*Below: a narrow street
in the Old Town
Bottom: the cathedral façade*

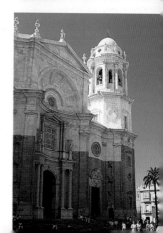

Maps
on pages
69 & 72

*Below: beach-goers
in the Bay of Cádiz
Bottom: Castillo de San Marcos in Puerto de Santa María*

an excellent collection of paintings including works by Zurbarán and Murillo. Not far away, the *Cortes* monument in **Plaza de España** ❼ commemorates the liberal constitution of 1812.

Heading towards the centre there is a fantastic view over the city from the **Torre Tavira** ❽, the watchtower of an 18th-century mansion (daily 10am–6pm). A little further west the **Oratorio de San Felipe Neri** ❾ (guided tours only) is a shrine to liberalism, as it was here that the first *Cortes* was held in 1812. It is also worth seeing for Murillo's fine *Immaculata* at the high altar.

The city tour ends back in Plaza de San Juan de Díos, overlooked by the classical facade of the town hall. If you have timed your tour well, you could take advantage of one of the traditional fish restaurants nearby; alternatively there are some good shops in the pedestrian zone at the rear.

BEYOND CADIZ

The bridge spanning the Bay of Cádiz (3.4km/2.1 miles in length) leads to the northwest and **Puerto de Santa María** (pop. 64,000), a typical southern Andalusian town and the main harbour for the export of the region's agricultural produce. A fun way to travel between Cádiz and Puerto de Santa María is via the ferry. It is worth making a detour to view this pretty town, for the 13th-century **Castillo de San Marcos** as well as the excellent fish restaurants.

If you make it this far, add another 21km (13 miles) to your itinerary by taking in **Sanlúcar de Barrameda**, attractively positioned at the mouth of the Río Guadalquivir. Take a walk along Paseo de Calzada to the gently flowing river, lined by fish restaurants, and look across to the Coto de Doñana nature reserve (*see pages 11 and 36*; ferry connection available).

Overlooking the roofs of the Old Town is the Gothic Castillo de Santiago, the former residence of the dukes of Medina Sidonia. A little lower down is a 14th-century Mudéjar church. While you are here, don't miss the opportunity to sample the local sherry.

6: White Villages of the Sierras

Serranía de Ronda and Sierra de Cádiz: Ronda – Puente Arabe – Setenil – Olvera – Grazalema – Arcos de la Frontera

Scattered around in the triangle between Sanlúcar de Barrameda in the west, Tarifa in the south and Ronda in the northern uplands lie the villages known as *los pueblos blancos* or 'the white villages' on account of the dazzling whiteness of the interlinked blocks of houses. Nestling on the hillsides, the houses cluster around the church. From a distance, the compact, gleaming white villages look like fields of snow on dark mountainsides. The tones of white change throughout the day – a yellowy tinge in the morning sun, pure white at midday and, as the sun sets, a bluish shadow descends over the *pueblos blancos*. They are a world apart, well away from the bustling throngs on the beaches of the nearby Costa del Sol.

RONDA

The town of ★★★ **Ronda** (pop. 34,000) lies in an impressive position on a steeply dropping rocky plateau, split asunder by a very narrow 100-m (325-ft) deep gorge, known as El Tajo. The southern part of the town, the Ciudad, consists of the Old Town, which was founded by the Arabs.

Map on page 69

Star Attraction
• Ronda

> **In praise of lime**
> The gleaming white *pueblos blancos* that characterise the Andalusian landscape are practical in origin, as the natural, unslaked lime that covers them protects against decay. It gives the walls solidity, its sterilising qualities guarantee cleanliness and the reflecting whiteness helps reduce the power of the sun. There is a good supply of lime in the vicinity. Lumps are piled up and burnt in a heap, and the remaining powder is then washed on to the walls every year. The Spanish term for this process is *enlucir* (to lighten).

Ronda and the Tajo Gorge

Map
on page
69

Below: Ronda's Old Town
Bottom: the bullring is the
oldest in Spain

North of the gorge is the 16th-century 'new' town, El Mercadillo. The 98-m (320-ft) high **Puente Nuevo** (built from 1784 to 1793), which links both parts of the town, is Ronda's main attraction. Two older bridges span the Tajo lower down the hillside where the terrain is flatter: the **Puente Romano**, which was rebuilt in the early 17th century, and the **Puente Arabe**, which has Moorish origins but has also been rebuilt.

THE OLD TOWN

While day-to-day life unfolds in El Mercadillo, tourists are inevitably drawn across the Puente Nuevo into the Old Town, right into Calle Tenorio and on to Plaza del Campillo, from where there is a fine view over the valley.

A narrow alley leads first to the ★ **Palacio de Mondragón** (Monday to Friday 10am–7pm, Saturday/Sunday 10am–3pm). A residence used by the Catholic Monarchs after the reconquest of the town, it still has some of the original Moorish mosaics and is now home to a local history museum. The alley then takes you on to **Plaza de la Duquesa de Parcent**. On the south side of the square lie the scant remains of the **Alcazaba**, while to the north stands **Santa María la Mayor**, which was built on the foundations of the mosque. Enter the church through the bell tower, originally the minaret. The mosque's prayer niche can be seen in the vestibule. Behind the church is a shady square with some souvenir and antique shops.

On the main street, Calle Armiñán, turn back to the Puente Nuevo. Just before the bridge a road leads steeply downhill, with the **Casa del Rey Moro** on the left-hand side. A flight of over 300 steps cut out of the rock in Moorish times leads down from the garden to a spring in the gorge. This building does not open its doors to the public although the gardens do (daily 10am–7pm).

A little further on the **Palacio del Marqués de Salvatierra** (daily 11am–2pm, 4–7pm, closed Thursday/Sunday afternoon; guided tours only; expect queues) welcomes visitors. Much of what we see today dates from the 18th century and there is a distinct colonial influence shown in some unusual images of South American indigenous people on the facade.

Star Attraction
• Ronda and surroundings

FURTHER SIGHTS

Return to the new town via the **Puente Arabe**. Down below are the **Baños Arabes**, an Arab baths complex (*circa* 1300), while to the right, on the edge of town, stands the **Espíritu Santo** church (16th century). If you walk via the panoramic viewing terraces, the **Alameda de Tajo**, to **Plaza de España**, there is a spectacular view of the Old Town, the gorge and the 18th-century bridge.

STAR PUEBLOS

Take the C4221 from Ronda past the steep mountain slopes and lush cork and chestnut oak forests of the Sierra de Grazalema to visit some of the finest of the 'white villages'. ★ **Setenil** has an extra attraction: some dwellings, only very few of which are still inhabited, were cut out of the tufa rock on the banks of the Río Setenil and have natural rock roofs.

Standing out clearly 10km (7 miles) further on above the C4222 is the dramatic silhouette of ★ **Olvera**. The greenish brown landscape surrounds

> **Bullfighting**
> Ronda is proud of its status as the birthplace of bullfighting. It was here in the 18th century that the Romero family first laid down the rules that remain valid to this day. The arena here, inaugurated in 1784, is the oldest in Spain. Part of the complex houses a **museum** (daily 10am–7pm; summer until 8pm) with posters, photographs, daggers and costumes belonging to famous toreadors. A *corrida goyesca* (so-called because the toreadors and some of the audience dress in the 18th-century costumes of Goya's paintings) is held in September, during the annual fair.

A view from Olvera's castle

Below: Olvera's traditional
white houses and church
Bottom: dominos in Ubrique

a fringe of traditional white houses, dominated by a huge church with two bell towers – a plain but solid place of worship, built on the ruins of a mosque. Visitors may climb the tower in what remains of the adjacent Almohad castle.

★ **Grazalema** lies at the foot of a huge rock. Narrow winding lanes lead past the facades of the white houses, in many cases embellished with extravagant wrought-iron on the windows and doors. Grazalema is well known for its traditional esparto grass weaving and wickerwork.

THE FIRST NATURAL PARK

After crossing the Puerto del Boyar mountain pass (1,103m/3,618ft), you will first come to the village of Benamahoma on the right, followed soon after by **El Bosque**. Instead of taking this route you could make a short detour, just before Grazalema, where the C3331 branches off to the south. The small town of **Ubrique** is then a further 21km (13 miles). It is noted for its leather processing and saddleries.

The ★★**Parque Natural de la Sierra de Grazalema** (51,700 hectares/125,280 acres), the first natural park in Andalusia, was opened in 1984. Because of its scenic appeal – gorges and caves – it is very popular with walkers. The vegetation here is dominated by large expanses

of cork and holm oaks, as well as native fir trees (*Abies pinsapo*) and Portuguese oaks. Fighting bulls for the *corridas* are bred on the meadows among the oak forests. Mountain goats can still be seen foraging in the park, which is also home to a wide variety of birds of prey, including buzzards and griffon vultures.

Star Attraction
• Parque Natural de la Sierra de Grazalema

ARCOS DE LA FRONTERA

From Ubrique take the 14-km (9-mile) country road to El Bosque and then continue westward as far as ★ **Arcos de la Frontera** (pop. 28,000). The great double crag of limestone above the Río Guadalete behind the town at 160m (525ft) can be seen from many miles away. Several towns in this area carry the suffix *de la Frontera* meaning 'by the border'. Not surprisingly, during the *reconquista*, the dividing line between Christian and Moorish territories changed constantly.

Below: leatherware in Ubrique
Bottom: Ubrique locals

Arcos is a superb example of a *pueblo blanco*. After the reconquest of the town by Alfonso X in 1264, a number of splendid palaces and mansions were built here, including the ★ **Casa del Conde de Águila** with its fine Mudéjar portal. If you follow signposts to the Parador Nacional, you will eventually come to the town's main square, the **Plaza del Cabildo**.

At one end of the square is the **Iglesia de Santa María de la Asunción**, which has an interesting plateresque portal and splendid choir stalls. The church tower, complete with tiled decorations, was built in the 18th century and formed the last stage in the construction of the building. It is possible to see the battlements of the ruined Moorish *castillo* (not open to the public) from outside the *parador*.

The **mirador** affords a magnificent view over the valley and deep into the surrounding mountainous countryside. Continue through the tangle of alleyways and on to the late-Gothic **Iglesia de San Pedro** and the viewing terraces perched on the edge of the cliff.

The N342 continues on to **Jerez de la Frontera** (*see page 88*).

Map
below

7: Across Andalusia

La Calahorra – Guadix – Purullena – Baena – Antequera – El Torcal – Osuna – Alcalá de Guadaira

This varied route passes through a series of striking landscape formations and historic towns as it crosses the Andalusian interior. Start out from Almería and climb to the Guadix plateau, then cross the north-western foothills of the Sierra Nevada and descend into the Genil valley and continue to Granada. Follow the Genil basin as

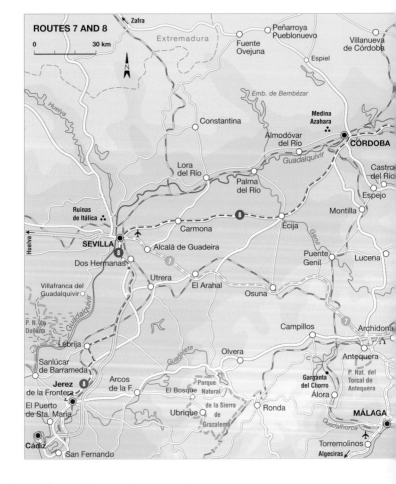

ROUTES 7 AND 8

0   30 km

N

Zafra
Extremadura
Peñarroya Pueblonuevo
Fuente Ovejuna
Espiel
Villanueva de Córdoba
Emb. de Bembézar
Medina Azahara
Constantina
Almodóvar del Río
Guadalquivir
CÓRDOBA
Huelva
Castro del Río
Lora del Río
Palma del Río
Espejo
Ruinas de Itálica ∴
Carmona
Écija
Montilla
Huelva
SEVILLA
Alcalá de Guadaira
Genil
Dos Hermanas
Puente Genil
Lucena
Villafranca del Guadalquivir
Utrera
El Arahal
Osuna
P. N. de Doñana
Guadalquivir
Campillos
Archidona
Lebrija
Olvera
Antequera
Sanlúcar de Barrameda
Guadalete
P. Nat. del Torcal de Antequera
Jerez de la Frontera
Arcos de la F.
Parque El Bosque Natural
Garganta del Chorro
Álora
El Puerto de Sta. María
de la Sierra de
Ronda
MÁLAGA
Cádiz
Ubrique
Grazalema
Guadalhorce
San Fernando
Torremolinos
Algeciras

far as Antequera and then descend into the Guadalquivir lowlands via Osuna before reaching Seville.

The best way to make this tour is by car; it is possible by bus or train but it will take a long time and connections may be inconvenient.

FOLLOWING THE RIVER

Take the N340 from Almería following the Río Andarax across the fertile Huerta de Almería with its expanses of orange and lemon groves. Turn

Opposite: midday shade under an olive tree

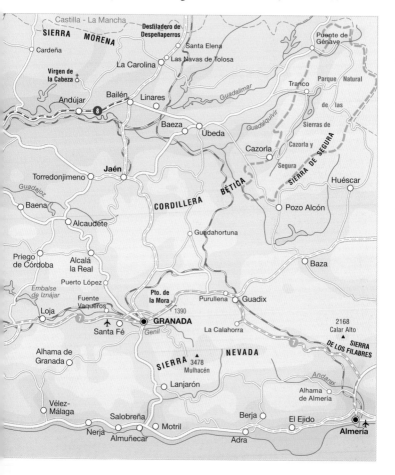

Map
on pages
80–81

Cave Dwellings
The *barrio troglodita* in Guadix has a cave museum, the Cueva Museo, which demonstrates aspects of subterranean life. If you fancy finding out for yourself, there's also a cave hotel (Cuevas Pedro Antonio de Alarcón, tel: 958 66 49 86).

Below: Cave Museum sign in Guadix
Bottom: Purullena ceramics

left along the N324 up to the Guadix plateau. After 94km (58 miles), there is a turning to ★ **La Cala-horra**. The **castle** of the same name, perched on a hill, will soon become visible. From the exterior it looks a dour and impregnable structure, but inside there is an unexpectedly elegant Renaissance patio. The two-storey arcades that surround the courtyard are adorned with the Mendoza coat-of-arms, garlands of pomegranates and an encircling inscription.

CAVES AND CHURCHES

Some 13km (8 miles) further on is ★★ **Guadix,** the birthplace of the founder of Buenos Aires, Pedro de Mendoza (1487–1537). The town (pop. 20,000) lies at the heart of a 1,000-m (3,280-ft) high valley basin. Severe erosion has resulted in the formation of dome-shaped rocks, bare and desolate. Only the narrow strip of green beside the river stands out against the barren, reddish loam soil.

Guadix is best known for its *barrio troglodita* or **Barrio de Santiago**, to give it its correct name. The cave dwellings here – some 2,000 of them – have been excavated from the soft loess, but often all that is visible are whitewashed porches and chimneys. The houses are connected up to the water and electricity network and most have mod-

ern conveniences. Many of the cave dwellers are happy to allow visitors in for a quick look in return for a small sum of money.

Guadix was one of the most important towns in the Moorish kingdom, hence the town wall and fortress, the **Alcazaba**, which was modified on several occasions before the 16th century. Not far from the Alcazaba stands the **Iglesia de Santiago** (16th century) monastery church with Carlos V's coat-of-arms prominently displayed above the Plateresque entrance. Inside is an admirable Mudéjar ceiling.

Leave the arcaded **Plaza Mayor** by the passage at the eastern end to reach the **Catedral** (1510–1796), built on the site of the mosque. Behind the baroque west facade is an extraordinarily effective triple-nave interior, resembling a miniature version of Málaga cathedral.

PURULLENA POTTERY

Only 6km (4 miles) beyond Guadix there is another town famous for its cave dwellings, **Purullena**. Visitors also come here to buy pottery from the shops and studios that line the main street. From the highest point on the climbing road, **Puerto de la Mora** (1,390m/4,560ft), there are some magnificent views over the valley to the Sierra Nevada beyond.

GRANADA TO CORDOBA

This alternative route involves following the N432, linking **Granada** and **Córdoba** (approximately 170km/105 miles). The road initially takes the Puerto López pass (900m/2,950ft), and the first town of any size is **Alcalá la Real**, where the houses are clustered around a steep hill crowned by the **Fortaleza de la Mota**. This fortress, founded in the 10th century by the Moors, was adapted for Christian use after the reconquest. The road then crosses the olive groves in the south of Jaén Province, the largest olive-growing area in the world.

A turn to the left at Alcalá la Real takes you

Below and bottom: hearth and home Guadix-style

Map on pages 80–81

Below: Federico García Lorca, who was born in Fuente Vaqueros
Bottom: Lorca's crib in his birthplace

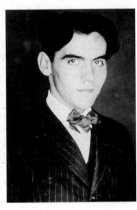

to ★ **Priego de Córdoba**, a town made wealthy by the silk industry in the 18th century. It is famous for its baroque architecture: the churches of **La Asunción** and **La Aurora** are particularly outstanding and the Fuente del Rey is a magnificent fountain in the same ornate style.

A little further along the same road, copper, brass and bronze workshops flourish in the town of ★ **Lucena**, which was once a completely Jewish community.

Back on the road to Córdoba, **Baena** is well known for its Holy Week festivities and also for the vineyards where grapes for the famous Montilla wines are grown.

Pass through Castro del Río, just before the picturesque little town of **Espejo** (literally 'mirror'). The 15th-century castle here was built by the dukes of Osuna. A short way further on, at the foot of a mountain ridge, the Guadalquivir valley will come into view.

ON TO SEVILLE

If you chose not to take the alternative route – or made the detour and returned to Granada – continue on the N342 westwards to Seville, initially following the Río Genil.

In **Santa Fé**, on 17 April 1492, Christopher Columbus received from Queen Isabela the contract that authorised him to seek the western sea route to India. The town grew out of the rectangular, walled encampment, from where the siege of Granada was masterminded. At the intersection of the main roads stands the church. The three surviving town gates were renewed in the 18th century.

DETOUR TO FUENTE VAQUEROS

Near the airport a country road turns off to **Fuente Vaqueros** (a detour of 5km/3 miles), the birthplace of the poet Federico García Lorca, who was killed by the Nationalists in August 1936, early in the Spanish Civil War. The house where this celebrated literary figure was born has been a museum since 1986 (Tuesday to Sunday 10am–3.30pm, 4–7pm). The living rooms, furnished with family belongings, provides some insight into the everyday life of the rural middle classes around 1900. Temporary exhibitions are held on the first floor.

Star Attraction
• **Antequera's Old Town**

ANCIENT ANTEQUERA

The town of **Loja** (pop. 21,000) lies to the right of the main road in the Genil valley. The ruins of a Moorish fortress with a well-preserved cistern *(aljibe)* inside can be seen on the hilltop. Work on the **San Gabriel** church, modelled on Granada cathedral, began in 1552.

A little further west, just beyond Archidona, a typically Andalusian town set on a mountain slope, lies the attractive provincial town of ★★ **Antequera** (pop. 40,000). The origins of this valley settlement are prehistoric, as the nearby dolmens testify. The Megalithic burial grounds known as **Cueva de Viera**, **Cueva de Menga** and **Cueva del Romeral** date from 2500BC (Tuesday to Friday 10am–2pm, 3–5.30pm, Saturday/Sunday 10am– 2pm). They lie to the northeast of town, the furthest being 4km (2 miles) away.

Antequera's Old Town, consisting of some interesting palaces built in the 16th–18th century, is under a preservation order. Pay a visit to the

Below: statue in Loja
Bottom: Antequera

Map
on pages
80–81

Below: Arco de los Gigantes in Antequera
Bottom: grazing near the Garganta del Chorro

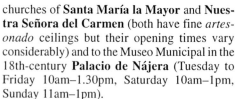

churches of **Santa María la Mayor** and **Nuestra Señora del Carmen** (both have fine *artesonado* ceilings but their opening times vary considerably) and to the Museo Municipal in the 18th-century **Palacio de Nájera** (Tuesday to Friday 10am–1.30pm, Saturday 10am–1pm, Sunday 11am–1pm).

It is also worth strolling up to the ruins of the Moorish castle, approached through the magnificent 16th-century **Arco de los Gigantes**.

NATURAL SPECTACLES

To the south of Antequera lies the dark, limestone **El Torcal** plateau, now protected as the ★ **Parque Natural del Torcal**, which covers an area of 20 sq.km (7½ sq.miles). Initially take the C3310 through an eroded landscape that is a bizarre sight with layered forms like mushrooms or hats towering beside the marked footpaths. The best time of year to visit the nature reserve here is during the spring when the orchids are in flower.

An even greater natural spectacle nearby is the ★★ **Garganta del Chorro** (on the C337 between Antequera and Alora). The foaming green waters of the Río Guadalhorce cut through a narrow 200-m/650-ft gorge. The torrent can be seen clearly from the railway line between Málaga and Antequera. Footpaths – especially the **Camino del Rey**

– permit access to the rock walls on both sides of the gorge, making for some exhilarating walks.

OSUNA

Our route from Antequera continues along the N334 towards Seville. ★ **Osuna** (pop. 17,000) was once the home of the powerful dukes of Osuna. In the 16th century they built the collegiate church of **Santa María de la Asunción** as their own burial chamber (Tuesday to Sunday 10am–1.30pm, 4–7pm). Most of them are buried in the pantheon called the Panteón Ducal. The church has a fine collection of paintings, including many by José de Ribera *(1591–1652)*, such as *The Crucifixion* and the *Martyrdom of St Bartholomew*.

To the east of the church stands the old University (1548), built in Renaissance style. It is now used as a school. Osuna has a number of fine palaces under preservation orders: the Palacio del Marqués de la Gomera (Calle San Pedro), the Palacio de los Cepeda (Plaza Mayor) and the former palace of justice (Calle Caballos).

ALCALA DE GUADAIRA

Next you pass through El Arahal before reaching **Alcalá de Guadaira** (pop. 53,000). The fortress here, high above the Río Guadaira, was built by the Almohads to defend their capital, Seville. It was modified in the 14th–15th century, but is still essentially the same huge and powerfully built structure that the Almohads intended.

Gitanos (gypsies) live in caves at the foot of the fortress. A large grain store beneath the castle is said to have kept Seville supplied with bread. The long, narrow town with its whitewashed houses has some interesting churches.

The ochre-coloured river sand *(albero)* that is scattered over the paths and squares in the parks of Seville every spring is dredged at Alcalá de Guadaira. The town is also well known in the region for its delicious pastries.

Continue along the N334, the main road to Seville (428km/265 miles from Almería).

Star Attraction
• Garganta del Chorro

Below: Alcalá de Guadaira, castle detail
Bottom: in the Parque Natural del Torcal

Bodega Tours
Most *bodegas* in Jerez de la Frontera organise guided tours on weekdays. The visits include a full explanation of the cultivation methods and the production process (10.30am–12.30pm). In the grounds of the González Byass *bodega* is a small chamber constructed out of steel by Gustav Eiffel who designed the Eiffel Tower.

8: Along the Guadalquivir

Jerez de la Frontera – Santa María de la Defensión – Lebrija –Carmona – Écija – La Carlota – Bailén

This route runs through the Guadalquivir valley from Jerez de la Frontera via Seville and Córdoba on to Bailén. It explores a wealthy agricultural region, several important historic sights in southern Spain, including some real delights. Allow for at least one overnight stop.

JEREZ DE LA FRONTERA

★★ **Jerez de la Frontera** (pop. 187,000) is the largest town in Cádiz Province and a busy commercial centre. It lives almost exclusively from its world-famous wines. Wherever you go in the town, you will see the impressive 'cathedrals of wine', the *bodegas*, or cellars, belonging to the large sherry producers.

A number of other buildings near the *bodegas* are also worth visiting, although it has to be said that Jerez doesn't have too many other places of tourist interest. It was originally the Moorish town of Xerox, conquered in 1264 by Alfonso X, and fought over for many years. Like many towns and villages in the region it was given the suffix *de la Frontera*. meaning 'by the border'.

Stable at the Royal Andalusian School of Equestrian Art

JEREZ HIGHLIGHTS

Start your tour of the town at **Plaza de los Reyes Católicos**, where you will see an equestrian statue dedicated to General Miguel Primo de Rivera who was born here in 1870, and whose dictatorship lasted from 1923 to 1930. The pedestrianised zone leads to the late-Gothic church of **San Miguel** (circa 1430). Inside is an elaborate altarpiece based on a design by Martínez Montañés (1625).

At the highest point in the town stands the **Alcázar**, built during the Almohad era – remarkably the mosque inside has survived. The brick structure with an octagonal dome is a rare example of palace mosque (12th century).

From the rear of the Alcázar you will see the **Colegiata del Salvador**, often called the cathedral, which was built on the foundations of a mosque. The present building with its huge open staircase dates mainly from the 18th century. What is remarkable here is the extended buttressing in a baroque building. The unusual painting in the treasury entitled *The Sleeping Girl* is credited to Francisco de Zurbarán.

Continue to the right towards **Plaza de la Asunción**, around which stand the former town hall (16th century) and the church of San Dionisio. The latter dates originally from 1430 but later underwent a baroque transformation.

SCHOOL FOR HORSES

The ★ **Real Escuela Andaluza del Arte Ecuestre** in Avenida Duque de Abrantes offers you the chance to experience the thrills of the Spanish Riding School. The thoroughbred Carthusian horses are relatives of the famous Lippizaners, usually associated with the Viennese school of classical horsemanship.

Dressage performances are staged every Thursday from March to October at 11am (public holidays excepted) and also on Tuesday at noon, in the school's vast riding hall (tel: 956 30 77 98 for further details). On other mornings you may be allowed in to watch the rehearsals and training sessions, which can be almost as interesting.

Star Attraction
• Jerez and its bodegas

Below: touring Jerez
Bottom: dressage performance

Map on pages 80–81

EL PUERTO DE SANTA MARIA

To the south-west of Jerez is the pleasant little port of **El Puerto de Santa María**, also ringed with *bodegas*, some of which may be visited. The port exports large amounts of sherry and has obviously flourished through the trade. There's an unobtrusive castle, but for visitors, the most interesting part is the seafront promenade called the **Ribera del Marisco**, lined with bars and restaurants serving good fresh seafood.

Below: a famous brand
Bottom: Santa María
de la Defensión

CARTHUSIANS AND CHRONICLES

About 5km (3 miles) to the east of Jerez is the Carthusian monastery called ★ **Santa María de la Defensión**, one of the region's architectural gems. It owes its origins to a private endowment in 1463. The magnificent portal, resembling a Roman triumphal arch, was the work of Andrés de Ribera (16th century). The late-Gothic church was given a baroque facade in the 17th century, but the earlier cloisters have survived. The Carthusian horses that you can see performing in the Jerez Riding School owe their name and origin to this monastery, where for many years the monks ran a stud farm.

Continue along the NIV. When you reach El Cuervo, consider making a detour to **Lebrija**. The town (pop. 29,000) is set between cotton fields

and canals that control water levels in the Guadalquivir marshes. A Moorish castle, now ruined, once occupied the hilltop. The view from the summit encompasses the fertile, alluvial plain.

The main church in the town, **Santa María de la Oliva**, is of special interest. Set into the wall above the north portal is a Visigothic stele. The triple-nave interior still retains some 13th-century features, namely the ornate ribbing in the side aisle domes. The east side was rebuilt during the Renaissance. Alonso Cano created the Madonna sculpture that adorns the high altar.

The monument on the main square honours one of the town's famous sons, Antonio de Nebrija (1441–1522). He was a chronicler in the service of the Catholic Monarchs and produced the first grammar of the Castilian language. At the height of the empire's territorial expansion, the new Spanish state was seeking a national identity and this meant a unified faith and a shared language, *Castellano*.

CARMONA

After this detour, continue along the A4 /NIV through large expanses of cereal and cotton fields, only occasionally interrupted by isolated farmhouses or *cortijos*.

Just before you enter ★★ **Carmona** (pop. 24,000), a signpost points left to the **Necrópolis Romana**, which was in use between the 2nd and 4th century AD. Archaeologists have uncovered thousands of tombs here. This 'city of the dead' lay beside the ancient long-distance Hispalis–Corduba route. It is still possible to see the walls of the crematorium, discoloured by the heat of the fires. The entrance is in the northeast corner close to the spot where the partially-excavated amphitheatre – thought to date from the Augustan period – is situated.

THE OLD TOWN AND THE FORTRESSES

Carmona's Old Town is partly enclosed by a medieval wall. Outside it is the church of **San**

Star Attraction
• **Carmona**

Below: sign to Carmona's necropolis
Bottom: enjoying tapas in Jerez

Map
on pages
80–81

Parador de Carmona
Like most of Spain's chain of *paradors*, the one in the Alcázaba is beautifully situated with fine views, and combines historic atmosphere with the usual modern conveniences. Contact Parador de Carmona, Calle Alcázar, Carmona, 41410 Sevilla, tel: 954 14 10 10.

Pedro with a bell tower modelled on the Giralda in Seville. Opposite San Pedro lies the **Puerta de Sevilla**, the town's main gate. It has Roman origins but was rebuilt by the Almohads. To the left you can see the remains of the **Alcázar de Abajo**, a Moorish castle.

If you continue uphill, you will come to the Plaza Mayor. Close by in Calle Salvador is the **Ayuntamiento** (Town Hall) with an interesting Roman floor mosaic. About 100 m/yds from the main square stands the **Iglesia de Santa María**, which in the 15th century replaced the Almohad mosque. An attractive patio has survived from the earlier building.

There are several routes through the maze of narrow streets in the Old Town, where structural details on the simplest of houses help to bring back to life important moments in Carmona's history. Most roads lead up to the *parador* in the grounds of the **Alcázaba de Arriba**. This second fortress occupies the highest point in the town. Only the surrounding walls remain from the Moorish fortress, which was modified by the Castilian king, Pedro I, in the 14th century. Because of this it is also known as the **Alcázaba de Rey Pedro**. A counterpart to the Puerta de Sevilla, the classical **Puerto de Córdoba** on the east side of the town indicates the direction in which this route continues.

Carmona's medieval wall

ECIJA

It is said that the apostle Paul preached to the faithful in ★ **Écija** (pop. 36,000) during Roman times. Remains of the town wall and the irregular street pattern are clues to the town's Moorish past. After its destruction in the earthquake of 1755, Écija was rebuilt in late-Baroque style. Situated in the heart of the Guadalquivir lowlands, it is reckoned to be one of the hottest places in Spain.

In the centre, remarkably endowed with monuments for such a small town, is the town hall and the long and narrow palm-shaded **Plaza de España**, where local people walk and talk in the relative cool of the evening.

A few yards to the northeast of the main square stands the **Palacio de los Marqueses de Peñaflor**, which now houses the municipal library (only the courtyard is open to the public). A balcony runs the full length of one wing overlooking Calle Caballeros. Other fine mansions such as the **Palacio de los Marqueses de Santaella**, the **Palacio de Valdehermoso** and **Palacio de Benameji** are also of interest.

As you stroll around the town you will come across countless fine Baroque facades, and the gleaming, tiled spires of Écija's many churches are always visible. In many buildings it is still possible to pick out the remains of original Mudéjar architecture, including in the **Iglesia de Santiago** (Calle de Padilla) and in the **Convento de San José** (Calle el Conde).

THE ROAD TO CORDOBA

As you continue along the NIV to Córdoba you will pass **La Carlota**, a village founded by German and Dutch colonists in the 18th century. The road then follows a northeasterly route running alongside the Río Guadalquivir, which you cross near Andújar. **Bailén** stands at a busy junction where roads from the north, south and southwest converge. The small town has an attractive pedestrianised zone but little else of real interest.

Star Attraction
•Écija

Below: Iglesia de Santiago in Écija
Bottom: Plaza de España

Map below

9: Across the Cordillera Bética

Almuñécar – the Alpujarras – Lanjarón – Trevélez – Jaén – Úbeda – Sierra de Cazorla

This route begins by the Mediterranean coast in the resort of Almuñécar and then heads inland into the mountains via Granada and Jaén. It crosses some of Andalusia's finest mountain scenery, namely the Alpujarras on the southern slopes of the Sierra Nevada, the Sierra de Cazorla and the Sierra Morena, plus the Guadalquivir depression in the east. This proposed route is one that should not be hurried. If you want to appreciate to the full the many natural beauty spots, allow yourself plenty of time, not least because of the road conditions. The Alpujarras alone need two days. The simplest way to cover the distance is by car, as bus services in the Alpujarras and the Sierra de Cazorla are thin on the ground.

INTO THE ALPUJARRAS

The N323 climbs steadily up to the little town of Vélez de Benaudalla. The route then passes through the Guadalfeo gorges, before ascending into the mountains. After 30km (18 miles) take a turning to Lanjarón, the gateway to the ★★**Alpujarras**.

The quiet, delightfully located spa town of **Lanjarón** (pop. 5,000) has been a popular destination for many years, mainly because of the curative powers of its spring water. Apart from the thermal bath operations, many people earn their living from bottling the mineral water, which is enjoyed throughout Andalusia. On a hill opposite the town lie the ruins of a Moorish fortress. Little of the original complex has survived, but the panoramic view over the bizarre mountain landscape of the Alpujarras is spectacular. The foothills of the Sierra Nevada receive plenty of rain so grapes, olives, oranges, lemons and almonds can be cultivated on the lower terraces.

ROUTE 9

0   20 km

La Carolina
Linares
Bailén
Baeza
Guadalimar
Torreperogil
Úbeda
Peal de Becerro
La Iruela
Jódar
Cazorla
Quesada
Mancha Real
Jaén
SIERRA DE CAZORLA
Guadalquivir
Guadahortuna
1040
Pto. de Onitar
Guadix
Granada
Genil
Pto. del Suspiro del Moro
860
SIERRA NEVADA
Sierra Nevada 3398
3478 Mulhacén
Pico de Veleta
Trevélez Yegen
Padul
Dúrcal
Capileira
Pampaneira
Lanjarón
LAS ALPUJARRAS
Ugíjar
Málaga
Guadalfeo
Vélez de Benaudalla
Salobreña
Motril
Almuñécar
Adra
Almería

SUGAR-CUBE HOUSES

Just before **Orgiva**, a winding but good mountain road climbs to some of the most delightful towns in the Alpujarras. The first stop is **Pampaneira**, a primitive-looking 'white village' at an altitude of 1,058m (3,470ft). Clinging to the hillsides like a staircase are the interlocking sugar-cube houses with flat-stepped roofs made from timber, slate and alumina, a feature typical of the Alpujarras. The two villages of **Bubión** and **Capileira**, slightly higher up, are built in the same style.

EUROPE'S HIGHEST ROAD

The highest mountain road in Europe crosses the Sierra Nevada to link Granada and Pampaneira, passing close to the summits of Mt Mulhacén (3,478m/11,411ft) and the Pico de Veleta (3,398m/11,148ft). The road is not always open, however, and should only be negotiated in a four-wheel-drive vehicle. Make enquiries locally or at the tourist office in Granada before setting out.

THE HAMS OF TREVELEZ

If you remain on the country road, you will come to **Trevélez**, the highest village in Spain (1,650m/5,413ft). The local speciality, air-dried ham (which comes from the local free-ranging pigs),

Star Attraction
• villages of the Alpujarras

Alpujarra Walks
The Alpujarras are an excellent region for walking tours. Basic maps can be obtained from the tourist information offices in Lanjarón and Pampaneira. An organisation in Pampaneira known as Nevadensis (tel: 958 76 31 27) arranges walking tours with guides.

Below: local Lanjarón crafts
Bottom: Trevélez landscape

Map
on page
94

Below: view of Jaen from Castillo de Santa Catalina
Bottom: Parador in the Castillo

is served in the simple restaurants by the viewing platform. Sit here and enjoy the spectacular view, which comes free of charge. On the other side of the road the village itself sits on a flank at the end of a ravine and looks even more primitive than those lower down the hillsides.

A WRITER'S INSPIRATION

Yegen, where the English writer Gerald Brenan (1894–1987) lived for many years, is a further 25km (16 miles). His reminiscences of the years he spent here are recorded in his book *South from Granada*. It was published in 1957, but if you take a look round this isolated mountain village, you will see that many of his descriptions remain just as accurate today as they were back in the 1950s. Brenan's earlier and most famous work, *The Spanish Labyrinth*, is considered one of the best studies on 20th-century Spain.

After 88km (55 miles) you reach **Ugíjar**; here you can choose whether you want to continue on to Almería, to cross the mountains to La Calahorra *(see Route 7)* or to continue with this route. If you choose the latter, you will have to return to the N323. After Dúrcal and Padul, you will need to negotiate the pass called the **Puerto del Suspiro del Moro** (Gate of the Moor's Sigh) (860m/2,821ft) before descending into the Genil valley.

JAEN

Beyond Granada you cross the southwestern foothills of the Cordillera Bética before entering olive country.

The town of ★ **Jaén** (pop. 110,000), at the foot of the Sierra de Jabaluz, can be divided into two parts. The modern town has few sights of any special interest, except for the **Museo Provincial** (Tuesday 3–8pm, Wednesday to Saturday 9am–8pm, Sunday 9am–3pm, closed Monday). Situated on the main street, Paseo de la Estación, it has an interesting collection of paintings, Roman mosaics and ceramics.

OLD TOWN SIGHTS

The **Old Town** is well worth exploring. The Paseo opens on to Plaza de la Constitución, and this extends through to the older part of town where the **Catedral** is situated. Work began on the building in 1540. The extravagant west facade, flanked by two tall towers, dates from the 17th century. The plateresque sacristy by Andrés de Vandelvira is an architectural masterpiece.

Overlooking the square in front of the cathedral are the **Ayuntamiento** (Town Hall) and the **Palacio del Arzobispo**. Take Calle Maestra into the quiet Old Town with its steep, narrow alleyways sheltered by the citadel and the Moorish **Castillo de Santa Catalina**, extended by the Christians after the reconquest in 1246. Part of the fortress has been transformed into a *parador*.

Pass the 15th-century **Arco de San Lorenzo** and follow Calle Aguilar to the church of **San Juan** at the end. On the right is the Mudéjar **Capilla de San Andrés**, which dates from the 16th century. Only a few yards away are the remarkable 11th-century **Baños Árabes**. This well-preserved complex of baths, with some perfect horsehoe arches, was discovered at the beginning of the 20th century beneath the **Palacio de Villardompardo**. As well as giving access to the baths, the palace houses a museum of arts and crafts (Tuesday to Friday 9am–8pm, Saturday and

Star Attraction
•Jaén

Influential Architect Andrés de Vandelvira, who designed the Cathedral sacristy, was an important figure in the development of the Early Spanish Renaissance style known as plateresque. More of his work can be seen in Úbeda *(see page 99).*

The ornate west facade of Jaén Cathedral

Maps
on pages
94 & 100

Sunday 9.30am–2.30pm, closed Monday and public holidays) and a collection of naive paintings.

Leave the Baños Árabes via Calle Uribes to reach **La Magdalena**, a quarter whose special qualities lie in the details, especially the Roman columns and Moorish washbasins scattered along the streets.

For a good look at the great swathes of the surrounding olive fields, take a drive along the bypass as you leave town.

BEAUTIFUL BAEZA

Below: olive groves
outside Jaén
Bottom: Plaza de los
Leones in Baeza

Leave Jaén on the N321 and head northeast to ★★**Baeza** (pop. 15,000). The Moorish origins of Baeza have disappeared beneath some 50 Renaissance palaces, built in warm, honey-coloured stone. Unlike most other Spanish towns, the churches are overshadowed by the splendid secular buildings.

At the end of the Calle San Pablo, where there are some magnificent palace facades, is the main square, Paseo de la Constitución. The **Ayuntamiento**, a splendid two-storey building dating from 1559, with some detailed carving around the main doorway, can be seen to the west in Calle Gaspar Becerra. The ruins of the **Convento de San Francisco** are nearby. Part of the church has been restored and is now used as a restaurant.

At the southern end of Paseo de la Constitución you will find **Plaza del Pópulo**, also known as **Plaza de los Leones** on account of the figures of lions incorporated into the central fountain. The **Archivo Histórico** (City Archives) are kept in what was once the abattoir. The **Audiencia**, or appeal court (1530), stands at the southeastern corner of the square.

Further round to the east stands the **Catedral de Santa María** overlooking the plaza of the same name (cut through on Cuesta de San Gil). A small, 13th-century Mudéjar portal can be seen on the west facade. The main entrance, however, and the interior are clearly Renaissance.

Perpendicular to the cathedral stands the 18th-century **Casa Consistorial Altas** (1511), the old Renaissance town hall, which has some splendid plateresque features. To reach the finest of the town's palaces, the **Palacio de Jabalquinto**, designed by Juan Guas, take Cuesta de San Felipe. The facade here contains elements of Mudéjar style, combined with late-Gothic and Renaissance influences. To the right of the palace lies the large campus for the 19th-century Old University, while the church of **Santa Cruz** opposite displays late Romanesque features.

UBEDA

It is clear from the uniform Renaissance style of its buildings that ★★★**Úbeda** (pop. 30,000) enjoyed its heyday during the 16th century. It is a far more lively place than Baeza. In 1975 the town was awarded 'model status' by the Council of Europe for the conservation of its historic monuments. The best place to start a tour is at the huge **Hospital de Santiago** ❶ (1562), designed by Andrés de Vandelvira. With its square bell towers and graceful Renaissance courtyard, it now houses a conference centre.

Continue along Calle del Obispo Cobos as far as Plaza de Andalucía, then turn right into Calle del Rastro. Further south on the left is the **Palacio de la Rambla** ❷. Two heraldic figures on the facade mark it out as a nobleman's residence.

Star Attractions
• Baeza
• Úbeda

Below and bottom: sculpture and interior detail at Úbeda's Hospital de Santiago

Maps on pages 94 & 100

Below: Palacio Vela de los Cobos
Bottom: Cazorla ceramics

Beside Plaza de San Pedro is the **Palacio del Conde de Guadiana ❸**, one of Úbeda's most striking palaces. Calle Real passes the **Palacio Vela de los Cobos ❹** before reaching Plaza del Ayuntamiento. From here it is a short distance to the impressive **Plaza de Vázquez Molina ❺**. Located in the vaults of the town hall is the **Casa de Cadenas ❻**, an interesting ceramics museum (Tuesday to Saturday 10am–2.30pm, 4.30–7pm, Sunday/public holidays 10.30am–2pm).

POTTERY CENTRE

Úbeda is famous for the pottery produced in the studios of master potter Paco Tito (Plaza del Ayuntamiento 12, near the town hall). Here you may watch the expert at work and buy anything you find particularly pleasing. Directly opposite stands **Santa María de los Reales Alcazares ❼**. The existing church structure dates from the end of the 15th century.

If you take a short detour along Calle de las Ventanas, you will come to the **Casa de las Torres ❽**, an unusual palace built in the 1530s. Return via Plaza de Vázquez Molina past the **Palacio de los Ortega ❾**, now a *parador*. A little further on is **San Salvador ❿**, a church built in the mid-16th century. Its facade is supported by two huge corner towers, while a relief above the portal shows the Transfiguration of Christ.

A lane leads northwards past **Casa de los Salvajes ⓫**, where two heraldic figures account for its name, which means 'House of the Savages'. On the west side of Plaza del Primero Mayo, a little further on, stands the **Old Town Hall ⓬**, with the **Iglesia de San Pablo ⓭** on the north side. The main entrance at one side – a stepped portal in late-Gothic style – was a later addition to this 14th-century place of worship.

SIERRA DE CAZORLA

To the east of Úbeda lies the **Sierra de Cazorla**, part of the **Parque Natural**

ROUTE 9 ÚBEDA

Sierras de Cazorla, Segura y las Villas, which covers a total of 214,336 hectares (529,049 acres), making it the biggest nature reserve in Andalusia. These mountain ranges constitute one of the largest enclosed forest areas in Spain.

Cazorla (pop. 10,000; 54km/34 miles from Úbeda), at an altitude of 826m (2,709ft), is a picturesque town at the foot of the mountain. The busy Plaza de Santa María lies at the heart of the settlement. Just 2km (1¼ miles) to the north is the village of **La Iruela**. The ruins of the Templar castle perched on a rocky peak are worth a visit.

The road now runs further into the Natural Park, which attains a maximum height of over 2,000m (6,500ft). The Sierras link the Cordillera Bética with the Sierra Morena in the north. The good stock of game in the park means that it has become a popular destination for hunters.

To conserve the waters of the Río Guadalquivir that rise in the Sierra de Cazorla, the **Embalse Tranco de Beas** reservoir, with a capacity of 1.1 million cubic metres and the largest of its kind in southern Spain, has been created.

It is possible to take mountain tours to the source of the Guadalquivir and to hike through the vast forest. The path network extends for 200km (128 miles). Guided walks are also available. For further information pay a visit to the tourist office at Torre de Vinagre, the first stop after Cazorla.

Star Attraction
• Sierra de Cazorla

Wildlife
If you are in the Parque Natural de Sierra de Cazorla at dawn or dusk, you may be lucky enough to see an otter. Other animals in the reserve include wild boar and mouflon, a breed of wild, large-horned sheep. There are also about 100 bird species here, so the park is extremely popular with bird-watchers.

Cazorla National Park

A Rich Legacy

Andalusia has some phenomenal cultural achievements to be proud of. Many different peoples have been attracted here, due to the region's strategically important position, to the Guadalquivir River being navigable deep inland, and to the presence of iron-ore deposits, plus the fertility of the soil. Each group of settlers then developed their own distinct cultural identity. The Moorish legacy has left a powerful imprint on the region's culture, while the influences of the Jewish communities and the gypsy fraternity are also important. All this can be seen in the art, architecture, literature and music of Andalusia, and in the ritual and the enthusiastic participation in the fiestas and processions.

The region's Moorish past can be seen in the architecture, town layouts and the decorative arts. As Arab culture gradually merged with that of Catholic Spain, a fascinating interplay in the arts emerged. The same is true for music. *Saeta*, a flamenco song adopted from Easter processions, has very clear Arabic influences. Andalusian flamenco and *sevillanas* are today an inspiration for pop groups and singing duos performing *a la gitana* (*gitano* means gypsy in Spanish), a musical form enjoyed throughout the world.

Art and Architecture

Three buildings represent the zenith of Moorish architectural development. The *Mezquita*, the mosque in Córdoba, dates from the Umayyad empire (756–1031). The oldest part was begun in 785. The two-storey construction supported by pillars and made up of circular and horseshoe-shaped arches was a totally new architectural concept for that era. That Byzantine craftsmen were involved in its completion is evident from the splendid mosaic-clad decor around the prayer niche (*circa* 965). Many of the techniques, decorative themes, and artistry, using ivory and precious metals, reached the Christian north via the Mozarabs (Christians living under Muslim rule).

Mudéjar style
The *Mudéjares* were the Moors who stayed on in the lands reconquered by the Christians. They were not persecuted or banished, but were called upon to apply their craftsmanship and skills in the service of Christ. The style that evolved was a blend of Christian and Islamic artistic traditions, most noticeable in ornamentation.

Islamic arabesques, Arabic calligraphy and geometric decorative features are often seen mingling with structural designs that are unmistakably Gothic. The Reales Alcazeres in Seville are a superb example of the Mudéjar style.

Opposite: beautiful Moorish geometric design
Below: horseshoe arches in the Mesquita, Córdoba

By far the most important legacy of the Almohads is the Giralda in Seville, the magnificent minaret of the great 12th-century mosque. It is said that the Moors valued it so much they wanted to destroy it rather than let it fall into Christian hands. Thankfully, we can still appreciate its beauty.

Nowhere has the sophisticated lifestyle of the Moors found better architectural expression than in the Alhambra, the Nasrid palace in Granada. Stucco ornamentation, colourful ceramic plinths and wooden ceilings with delicate inlay work could only be the work of ingenious craftsmen.

Although there was no specific ban on imagery, at least in the mosques, Islam generally avoids figurative representations, which can be seen as insulting to God the creator. It was this belief that gave rise to the arabesque, a highly sophisticated surface decoration of stylised, almost calligraphic-effect ornamentations on plant and flower themes. By covering structural elements with arabesques, architects succeeded in creating the impression of weightlessness. Any attempt to follow the flowing, intricate lines within the decoration will end in confusion.

Andalusian architecture is unimaginable without the colourful *azulejos* (glazed tiles). Introduced into Spain by the Moors, they decorate walls and plinths and give variety and colour to inner courtyards, patios and gardens.

Cortijos

The *cortijo*, Andalusia's traditional farmhouse, usually stands at the heart of a large agricultural estate. Country squires were excluded from the royal court, so in the 17th and 18th centuries they created their own mini-courts, or *cortijos*. The complex was fronted by a high wall with a large, ornamented portal at the centre. Adjacent to the other three sides were the residences of the property owner and the farm manager, accommodation for the workers and barns for storage.

Cortijos have become a symbol of the Andalusian landed gentry and an outward expression of the strict hierarchical society that still exists in rural areas. The most interesting of these mansions are to be found beside the Río Guadalquivir downstream from Córdoba.

Patio de los Leones in the Alhambra

ANDALUSIAN BAROQUE

Exuberant Andalusian baroque is associated with a period of economic depression and poverty during the 17th and 18th centuries, when it was accepted as a form of artistic expression designed to satisfy spiritual needs. Structural and creative embellishments in the chapel at the Hospital de la Caridad in Seville illustrate the baroque antithesis of piety and flamboyance. This contradiction is a basic principle of the style. The adoration of saints and the Virgin and a devotion to religious ceremony were ordained by clerics as an antidote to the counter-reformation, but they were also instrumental in glorifying power.

Below: Hospital de la Caridad in Seville
Bottom: Granada cathedral

CHURRIGUERISMO

The love of richly ornamented buildings culminated in what was known as *Churriguerismo*, after the Churriguera family of architects who covered structural skeletons with highly elaborate decorations. The exponents of this style, which is closely related to baroque, have left many fine examples throughout Andalusia, notably Alonso de Cano's facade for the cathedral in Granada (*circa* 1664) and López de Rojas' contribution to Jaén cathedral.

Leonardo Figueroa was responsible for completing the Hospital de los Venerables Sacerdotes in Seville. In the late 17th century. Francesco Hurtado Izquierdo, who worked on the Carthusian monastery in Granada, discovered effective combinations of semi-precious stones, marble and plaster. Sculptors such as Pedro de Mena and Pedro Roldán created images of saintly figures that are still appreciated today, andMartínez Montañés produced works of such perfection that he was nicknamed the 'god of wood'.

PAINTING

Some of the most celebrated exponents of Spanish baroque painting are of Andalusian origin. Diego de Velázquez (1599–1660), one of the best known of all Spanish painters, was born in Seville and set up his own studio there when he was only 19. Early works featured domestic scenes, their characters' faces reflecting those of ordinary working people. It was after visiting Italy and being influenced by Titian that his style changed and he concentrated on portraits at the court of Felipe IV. Perhaps his best-known works are *Las Meninas* (in the Prado, Madrid) and the *Rokeby Venus* (now in London's National Gallery).

Below and bottom: details of two works by Velázquez, Las Meninas and The Drunkards

Bartolomé Esteban Murillo (1618–82), who painted many variations of the *Immaculate Conception*, was also born in Seville, and the Museo de Bellas Artes there does justice to his work. He founded the Seville Academy in 1660 and became its first president. Pieces by one of his contemporaries, Juan de Valdés Leal, have recently been re-assessed after an exhibition at the Madrid Prado. Some of his macabre paintings can be seen in Seville's Hospital de la Caridad.

Another representative of the Seville school, well represented in the Museo de Bellas Artes and elsewhere is Francisco de Zurbarán (1598–1664), known as 'the painter of monks'.

Literature

Sensuality and reason, deemed to be irreconcilable during the Christian Middle Ages, enjoyed a successful synthesis in the literature of Al-

Andalus, notably in writings by Jewish poet and philosopher Salomón Ibn Gabirol (1021–57), Ibn Hazm (994–1064) and in the works of the mystic Ibn Al-Arabi (1165–1240). The Córdoba-born philosopher Ibn Ruschd (1126–98), known as Averroës, and the Jewish thinker Maimonides (1135–1204), had a lasting influence on Western thought, inspiring European philosophers from Spinoza to Schopenhauer.

THE GOLDEN AGE

The Golden Age for Spain corresponded with Seville's heyday. The main representative of the literary School of Seville was Fernando de Herrera (1534–97), known as El Divino, 'the divine one'. The sublime language of the baroque poet from Córdoba, Luis de Góngora (1561–1627), had many imitators. His contemporary, the Sevillian monk, Tirso de Molina (1583–1648), was the first to give the Don Juan legend literary form.

ROMANTICISM

Exponents of late 19th-century Spanish Romanticism include the Sevillian Gustavo Adolfo Bécquer (1836–70). Dramas by the Alvarez Quintero brothers, Serafín (1871–1938) and Joaquín (1873–1944), successfully reflected the Andalusian *zeitgeist*. Following in the footsteps of Rubén Darío (1867–1916), who founded the *Modernismo* literary movement, came Juan Ramón Jiménez (1881–1958), winner of the Nobel Prize for Literature in 1956 and a leading light in the avant-garde poetry group, *Generación del 27*. Another member of the group was Federico García Lorca (1898–1936), one of Granada's most famous sons *(see box)*.

CONTEMPORARY LITERATURE

Among contemporary writers, both Adelaida García Morales (b. 1947) and Antonio Muñoz Molina (b. 1956) have achieved a large measure of popularity beyond their Andalusian homeland,

Federico García Lorca
Lorca's lilting, rhythmic and colourful lyricism paints a picture of a highly traditional Andalusia. His dramas, *La Casa de Bernarda Alba*, *Bodas de Sangre* and *Yerma*, deal with the conflict between inflexible convention and the freedom of the individual. Many of his poems celebrate the *gitano* culture. Lorca, one of the most celebrated artists of his time, also gained a reputation as an essayist, speaker and producer. He was assassinated by a Nationalist firing squad soon after the outbreak of the Spanish Civil War.

Statue of the Jewish philosopher Maimonides

but they portray quite different images of the region. While Adelaida García Morales tries to express the mystery of the region's raw and elemental past, Muñoz Molina places emphasis on a 'personal' Andalusia, exploring pre-Islamic continuities of culture and religion.

Flamenco

> **Verdiales**
> *Verdiales* originated in the Málaga region. One of the oldest type of Andalusian music-making, it dates from the Morisco era (16th century) and has been handed down over the centuries, largely unchanged.

Andalusia is the home of flamenco. Although the music achieved widespread popularity towards the end of the 18th century, its roots can be traced back to the 15th century when gypsies from northern India arrived in Spain. They combined their musical traditions with an Andalusian musical heritage, which itself incorporated West Asian elements. Flamenco was the music of the disadvantaged – gypsies, poverty-stricken farmworkers and other minorities *(see pages 15–16)*.

In the middle of the 19th century, flamenco reached the bars, the *cafés cantantes*, which remained popular for decades. Aficionados nowadays get together in clubs *(peñas)* and also present their art at festivals and concerts.

The starting point for flamenco was the song *(cante)*. Dance *(baile)* and guitar accompaniment *(toque)* came later. Those familiar with the form can distinguish between *cante jondo* or 'singing from the depths' and *cante chico* 'light songs'.

All the early *coplas* or lyrics of *cante jondo* deal with the same themes: death, fate, freedom, incarceration and injustice. The underlying theme is a cry of despair without rebellion, a resigned protest. *Cante chico,* on the other hand, is about love, gaiety and the beauties of the countryside.

As flamenco increased in popularity, the *cante* developed a more artistic form. Basic forms such as *siguiriyas*, *soleares*, *bulerías*, *alegrías*, *tonás* and *tangos* have led to numerous other styles.

SEVILLANAS

The *sevillana* is popular throughout the region. As the name indicates, this is a folk dance that originated in Seville, but is danced today all over

Flamenco performance in Córdoba

southern Spain. Traces of Moorish and Oriental culture can be observed in the graceful but strictly regulated movements of the *sevillana*. Most typically the dance is preceded by an instrumental introduction and a sung section. In the *sevillana*, the dancers stop suddenly *(bien parado)* at the end of each *copla,* resuming dancing only after an instrumental interlude. The steps of each *copla* usually increase in intricacy and the dancers' castanets create complex counter-rhythms to their foot movements.

Festivals

Behind most Andalusian festivals lies a pilgrimage *(romería)* in honour of the Virgin Mary. Practically every village and urban *barrio* has its own *Virgen*. However, the religious significance of the event does not stop everyone from joining in what is in most cases a frenzied party. The *romerías* are therefore supported by *ferias*, flamenco festivals and grape-harvest celebrations. But other events in the religious calendar such as the May *Santa Cruz* festival and Corpus Christi are opportunities for the local population to take a break from everyday life.

The Spanish National Tourist Office will supply a detailed listing of festival events. The following is a selection of some of the best known.

Below and bottom: young festival participants

The Cofradías

It is the *cofradías* (brotherhoods) that give the *Semana Santa* celebrations their unique appeal. In Seville there are over 50 of these groups and their members, called *nazarenos* or *penitentes*, wear full-length robes and pointed hats with veils that allow only the eyes to peep out.

Every day six to eight brotherhoods make their way to the cathedral from their own parish church and then back again, accompanied by bands. Some 30 to 45 chosen *costaleros* (shoulder-bearers) carry the famous *pasos* – splendid floats depicting replicas of Christ on the cross or scenes from the Passion. Some brotherhoods also have a second *paso* with a statue of the Virgin Mary. Accompanied by the sound of *saetas*, mournful songs of devotion from the crowd, they make *Semana Santa* and unforgettable occasion.

Dressed the part

Carnaval in Cádiz. During the Middle Ages the Catholic church adapted a pagan festival as a way of letting off steam before the period of Lenten fasting. Fancy dress parades, flamenco and spectacular parades give the Cádiz *carnaval* a reputation as one of the most colourful in Spain. The highlight is the procession on Ash Wednesday.

Roméria a la Virgen de la Cabeza in Andújar (Jaén; last week in April). The Virgen de la Cabeza crowns the highest point of the Sierra de Andújar. In 1227 a shepherd boy is said to have found a madonna statue on this rocky peak. Thousands of pilgrims from all over Spain take part.

Feria de Abril in Seville (starts 10 days after Easter). Seville's great *feria*, there are daily parades of elegant riders and open carriages, and more than 1,000 *casetas,* or marquees, are set up so that Sevillanias can celebrate all night long.

Fiesta de las Cruzes in Córdoba (the first week of May). Large, flower-bedecked crosses *(cruzes)* are set up around town. The subsequent *Fiesta de los Patios,* when the city's inner courtyards, festooned with flowers, are opened up for viewing, lasts until mid-May. In the last week of May, after a week's break, the *feria* starts up again with more rounds of singing and dancing.

Feria de Pedro Romero in Ronda (first half of September). The main attraction is the Corrida Goyesca, when *toreros* honour the founder of modern bullfighting in costumes based on Goya's paintings. There's also a festival of flamenco.

Vendimia – grape harvest festivals in Jerez de la Frontera (early September). There are lively grape harvest festivals in many parts of Andalusia, but this is the biggest.

Fiesta de Verdiales in Málaga (28 December). Groups from all over the province gather in Málaga to celebrate this early form of flamenco.

SEMANA SANTA

Holy Week is celebrated throughout Spain with great fervour. In the south of the country, the solemn processions are followed by enthusiastic outpourings of joy and it is impossible not to be affected by it. By far the most spectacular events take place in Seville, where *Semana Santa* turns the city upside down. The great processions *(see box opposite)* begin on Palm Sunday and the entire inner city is blocked off for a week as the whole of Seville turns out to watch the processions. Everyone has their own favourite day, their favourite *paso* (float), their favourite Virgin.

The most important occasion is *madrugada*, the night spanning Maundy Thursday and Good Friday. The essence of the event is distilled into one huge festival as processions – each with about 2,000 *nazarenos* – begin their route shortly after midnight and end around midday.

Semana Santa in Málaga is not as famous as in Seville, but it is fascinating in its own way. Málaga's religious *confradías* (brotherhoods) also organise huge processions every day from Palm Sunday to Easter Sunday with splendid *tronos* or floats. The one in the city's Museo de la Cofradía de la Expiración weighs 5,500kg (nearly 5½ tons) and measures 68m (223ft) in length. As in Seville, every procession has its own ardent supporters. The *gitano* community follows the *Virgen de la O* and *Cristo en la Columna* on Easter Monday. Piety also finds visible expression in an act of compassion, as every year a convicted prisoner is pardoned and released, a custom which began under Carlos III in 1756.

Below: penitent in procession during Semana Santa
Bottom: men carrying the float for a religious celebration, Málaga

FOOD AND DRINK

Two important features shaped Andalusia's cuisine: short supply and Arab origins. The Moors introduced many spices and crops, such as sugar cane and rice. The preponderance of flour, bread, potatoes, pulses and eggs indicates a poor man's diet, although the dark, air-dried hams, such as *jamón serrano*, smoked hams and succulent olives are also important elements in southern Spanish fare. Andalusian cooks have proved to be extraordinarily inventive with the preparation of simple ingredients.

INVENTIVE DISHES

Meat is left to absorb the flavours of Arab marinades before being grilled as kebabs *(pinchos morunos)*, while kidneys are often left to soak in a good sherry *(riñones al jerez)*.

Garlic, chick peas and spinach *(espinacas con garbanzos)* may be an unusual combination, but when peppers, tomatoes and onions are the accompaniment any critics are usually silenced. Together with cucumbers and olive oil, the latter ingredients form the basis for *gazpacho,* a cold vegetable soup that has found favour throughout the world. Lemon juice and tuna are added to the same ingredients make an excellent salad, and the addition of puréed white bread makes a delicate cream (Córdoba's *salmorejo*). Potatoes are the filling for Spanish omelettes, *tortillas,* and eggs are often hard-boiled, halved and blended with spiced mayonnaise to make *ensaladilla rusa* (Russian salad). Meat and fish are usually cooked on the *plancha* – the hotplate – or grilled. Only rarely are sauces used. Double rations of garlic and olive oil are added to rabbit and seafood. The region's excellent goat's cheese is usually left in the same flavour-rich marinade.

SEDUCTIVE DESSERTS

The presence of almonds and honey in so many cakes and pastries is another sign of Arabic influence, although other syrupy specialities, often with biblical-sounding names such as *cabello de ángel* (angels' hair) and *tocino de cielo* (heaven's bacon) were developed in monasteries.

MEAL TIMES

Temperatures dictate how the day is structured and what is the best time to eat. Breakfast is usually restricted to something fairly light. Many people adjourn to a cafe-bar and enjoy a *tostada*, a toasted roll with olive oil, and a *café solo* (small black coffee), a *café cortado* (with a little milk) or a *café con leche* (coffee with plenty of hot milk). Lunch, *almuerzo*, is served between two and three o'clock in the afternoon, with the evening meal, *cena*, also eaten late. Good restaurants do not open until 9pm. The tasty snacks available in the *tapas* bars *(see below)* fill the gaps between meals.

Tasty tapas

Tapas are small, tasty portions of food that are sometimes served free with a drink. In Andalusia, these snacks have become real delicacies. *Riñones al Jerez* (kidneys in a sherry sauce), *albóndigas* (meatballs), *tortilla* (potato omelette) and *salpicón de mariscos* (seafood salad) are classic *tapas* snacks. *Salmorejo* is a cream made from the same ingredients as *gazpacho*, the famous cold soup, that is, tomatoes, peppers, cucumbers, hard-boiled eggs. *Huevas* (fish roe) is worth trying – not to be confused with *huevos* (eggs). Other specialities include *boquerones* (marinated anchovies), small fresh fish such as scampi, *pollo en salsa* (chicken stew) and marinated goat's cheese *(queso de cabra).*

VINO DE JEREZ

The region between Jerez de la Frontera, Sanlúcar de Barrameda and Puerta de Santa María is the home of Vino de Jerez or sherry.

The new wine is fermented in oak barrels and fortified with pure alcohol, up to 15 percent for *fino* or 18 percent for *oloroso*. It is then left to age, a process known as the *solera* system, which can take from three to nine years. During this time the sherry acquires its characteristic flavour. As many as six rows of butts are placed on top of each other. Over a period of time, the wine is gradually transferred from the top barrel to the bottom. Because sherries are blends of wines from different years, they are not designated by date.

There are two basic types: the light *fino* and the darker, golden *oloroso*. *Amontillado* is a type of *fino*. *Manzanilla,* from the Atlantic-coast town of Sanlúcar de Barrameda, is the finest of the *finos*. This old, light and very dry sherry has a pale colour, reminiscent of camomile tea, which is called *manzanilla* in Spanish. Classic sherry is always dry. Medium dry and sweet sherries are the result of blending.

One important factor in the maturation process is the layer of yeast bacteria or *flor*, a fluffy coating of scum, which protects the wine from oxidisation and lends the characteristic flavour. The *solera* system guarantees consistent quality year after year, as the lowest barrels always contain some of the older wine and this passes its flavour down to the new wine.

WINES

Montilla wines from the province of Córdoba are similar to sherries. Their alcoholic strength derives mainly from the grape (Pedro Ximénez). *Málaga*, a sweet, reddish-brown dessert wine, is produced in Málaga province.

Restaurant Selection

These suggestions for restaurants in the main centres are listed according to the following categories: $$$= expensive; $$= moderate; $= inexpensive.

Seville

Cueva, Plaza Elvira, Barrio Santa Cruz. Popular local restaurant. $$.

El Rincón del Pepe, Gloria 6, Santa Cruz. Pleasant atmosphere. $$.

La Albahaca, Plaza de Santa Cruz 12, tel: 954 22 07 14. Attractive decor. Imaginative food that mixes Andalusian, French and Basque influences. $$$

TAPAS BARS: The **Rinconcillo**, Pere Gil, and **La Giralda**, Mateos Gago are traditional, but out of the ordinary. The **Jabugo**, Castelar 1, is a good example of a modern version. Make your way through the Barrio Santa Cruz to the bars around Plaza Alfalfa and take your pick.

Córdoba

El Caballo Rojo, Cardenal Herrero 26, tel: 957 47 80 01. Good food, hence very popular. In the Judería. $$.

Almudaina, Campo Santo de los Martíres 1, tel: 957 47 43 42. Historic setting. Upmarket menu. $$.

Los Califas, Deanes 3. An elegant, traditional atmosphere. Cordoban specialities. $.

Córdoban specialities
If you're visiting Madinat al-Zahra near Córdoba, drop in at **Los Almendros**, Carretera de Trassierra, tel: 957 33 00 00 during the afternoon. In this excellent restaurant Cordoban specialities are served on the terrace from 1.30pm. Leave Madinat al-Zahra on the road to Ermitas, turn left at the petrol station; it's on the left after about 200m.

Try the **tapas** in the **Sociedad de los Plateros** (behind Plaza del Potro). *Salmorejo* (*see page 113*) is a speciality of Córdoba.

Gibraltar
Phone numbers are prefixed by 9567 if calling from Spain.
La Bayuca, 21 Turnbull's Lane, tel: 75119. One of Gibraltar's longest-established restaurants; international and Mediterranean food. $$.
Strings, 44 Cornwall Lane, tel: 78800. Small and cosy; bistro-style food. $$.

Granada
Carmen de San Miguel, Torres Bermejas 3, tel: 958 22 67 23. Nouvelle cuisine Andalusian-style. Small and expensive. $$$.
Cunini, Restaurante Marisquería, Plaza de Pescadería 14 (near the cathedral). Fish and seafood, *tapas*, good wines. $$.
Pilar del Toro, Hospital de Santa Ana 12 (near Plaza Nueva), tel: 958 22 38 47. Versatile restaurant for every occasion. Cafe, cocktail lounge with wicker furniture and palm trees, plus an upmarket restaurant serving Andalusian fare in a Renaissance palace. $$.
Posada del Duende, Duende 3 (near the Corte Inglés). Superb Grenadian specialities in an informal atmosphere. $$.
Sevilla, Oficios 12, tel: 958 22 12 33. Excellent long-established spot near the Capilla Real. Popular *tapas* bar, but classic meat and fish dishes also available. Try the *jamón con habas* (cured ham with broad beans). $$.
Zoraya, Panaderos del Albaicín 32, tel: 958 81 64 13. Popular destination for outings. Smart atmosphere. $$.
TAPAS BARS are concentrated around **Campo del Príncipe**, by Plaza Larga and in the Navas (Fogón) pedestrian passage. **Carrera del Darro** is a good

area for bars. Students get together around **Plaza Gran Capitán**.

Salobreña
El Peñon, Playa del Peñon, tel: 958 61 05 38. On a rocky cape by the sea below Salobreña. Take a dip and then enjoy one of the excellent fish dishes.

Málaga
Antonio Martín, Paseo Maritimo. One of the finest fish restaurants in Málaga. $$.
Astorga, Gerona 11, tel: 952 34 68 32. Lively, friendly, with good fish and meat dishes. Booking essential. $$.
El Chinitas, Moreno Monroy 4, tel: 952 22 09 72. Delicious food includes fish and lobster from the tank. $$.
There are recommended **tapas bars** to be found in **Pasaje Chinitas** at the upper end of Marques de Larios.

Ronda
Tenorio, Tenorio 1, tel: 952 87 49 36. Smart restaurant with tables amid nooks and crannies. Ambitious menu and small garden. In the Old Town. $$.
Doña Pepa, Plaza del Socorro, tel: 952 87 84 77. Traditional fare in an upmarket atmosphere. $.
Hermanos Macías, Pedro Romero 3, tel: 952 87 42 38. Traditional restaurant in a hotel. $
Pedro Romero, Virgen de la Paz 18, tel: 952 87 11 10. Touristy, but the food is good. It's opposite the bullring and *rabo do toro* (bull's tail) is the house speciality. $$.
There are lively **tapas bars** in Calle Pedro Romero.

Jaén
El Pilar del Arrabalejo, Millán de Priego 59. In the style of an Argentinian bar. $.
Méson Río Chico, Nueva 12. A lot of timber and whitewashed walls. Good *tapas*. $.

ACTIVE HOLIDAYS

With both an Atlantic and a Mediterranean coast, Andalusia is perfect for beach holidays and all kinds of watersports. Sailing enthusiasts will have plenty of marinas to choose from: Tarifa and the neighbouring beaches are windsurfing havens, and divers are inevitably drawn to the inshore waters near Almería.

Some unusual holiday combinations are also available. In Granada, for example, between December and April, not only are there the cultural aspects of the town to appreciate, but proximity to the Sierra Nevada means excellent skiing opportunities. A good road runs from Granada to the winter sports centre of Pradollano at an altitude of 2,100m (6,900ft). If you are looking for something out of the ordinary, then you can take lessons in hang-gliding or explore the uplands by mountain bike. The Sierra Nevada has something for everyone.

RIDING

Doma Vaquera is the name of a Spanish form of dressage, which experienced riders can practise in specialist riding schools. There are, however, many other opportunities for riding holidays in Andalusia, e.g. riding lessons and trail riding as part of half-day or whole-day tours, riding tours where you camp in tents and riding holidays on a *finca*.

Centro Ecuestre Epona, Carretera Madrid–Cádiz km 519, Carmona, Seville, tel: 908 155 359 and Actividades Ecuestres de la Subbética, Plaza Caballos 4–6, Córdoba, tel: 957 700 629 are two good riding centres, and more general information about equestrian activities is available from the Spanish National Tourist Office *(see page 120).*

GOLF

Andalusia is a golfer's paradise. The region has some 60 golf courses, most of them on the Costa del Sol. The Spanish National Tourist Office *(see page 120)* publishes a brochure with golf course listings. Alternatively, you can seek information from the Federación de Golf de Andalucía, Paseo del Pintor Sorolla 34/V , E-29016 Málaga, tel: 952 22 55 90.

WALKING

To the south of Granada lies the Alpujarras mountain range, an inhospitable but attractive region that is ideal for walking. In the foothills of the Sierra Nevada you have to seek out the footpaths for yourself, unless you have a guide. If you are planning more than one-day excursions, then you must make sure in advance that accommodation is available at your destination

For information about guided walks through the Sierra de Cazorla, ask at the tourist office in Jaén, Arquitecto Berges 1, tel: 953 22 27 37.

> **Rural pursuits**
> Walking tours and riding excursions amid wonderful scenery will sometimes be arranged for you if you book a holiday at a country house *(casa rural)*, through the Hoteles Rurales de Andalucía *(see page 123 for details)*.

FISHING

The many rivers that flow down from the Andalusian mountains provide anglers with some excellent waters. Fishing permits are available from ICONA, the body responsible for nature conservation, and can sometimes be arranged through local tourist offices.

PRACTICAL INFORMATION

Getting There

BY PLANE

Málaga is the busiest airport in the region, now equipped to receive 11 million passengers a year. Other international airports include those at Almería, Granada, Jerez de la Frontera and Gibraltar. The national carrier is **Iberia Airlines**, 29 Glass House Street, London W1R 6JU, tel: 020 7830 0011. Website: www.iberia. co.uk.

There are regular scheduled services and numerous low-cost charter flights from airports all over the UK and the rest of Europe, especially during the summer months.

The Sunday broadsheet newspapers are a good source of information about charter flights, many of which can be bought on-line. For example, www. easyJet.com or www.go-fly.com

BY CAR

To reach Andalusia by car, you can either take the inland route via Madrid or go along the coastal motorway via Barcelona *(Autopista del Mediterráneo)*. Tolls are payable on Spanish motorways. The price of petrol is roughly comparable with that in the UK, sometimes a little cheaper. *Gasolineras* (petrol stations) are open 24 hours a day on the main routes and sell super, unleaded *(sin plomo)* and diesel *(gas-oil)*.

Car drivers need to carry with them their national driving licence, vehicle registration documents and a Green Card. Third-party insurance is compulsory in Spain and drivers must obtain a Green Card from their insurance company. A bail bond should be supplied with it and is essential in the event of an accident.

The main traffic regulations are as follows: seat belts must be worn; the permitted blood alcohol level is five parts per thousand; drivers must not use mobile phones while at the wheel; and towing by private cars is not allowed.

The speed limit in urban areas is 50kmph (31mph), out of town 90kmph (56mph), on two-lane highways 100kmph (62mph), on motorways 120kmph (74mph). On-the-spot payment of fines is compulsory.

In the event of an accident the *Policia Municipal* are responsible for assisting in urban areas; elsewhere it is the *Guardia Civil de Tráfico*.

Emergency breakdown service: tel: 915 93 33 33. Check before you leave home whether your motoring organisation has a reciprocal agreement with its Spanish counterpart: **Real Automovil Club de España**, Calle Córdoba 17, Málaga, tel: 952 22 98 36.

BY COACH

Eurolines is the leading operator of scheduled coach services throughout Europe. It's a long journey, but a cheap way to get there. **Eurolines** tel: 0990 143219 and 020 7730 8235. Website: www.goby-coach.com

BY TRAIN

There are two possible routes: London – Paris – Barcelona – Málaga, or London – Paris – Madrid – Seville – Málaga. RENFE is the national rail operator and its high-speed trains (AVE) run between Madrid and Seville. **Eurostar** tel: 0990 186186. Website: www.eurostar.com.

If you want real ease and comfort (at a price) it's worth checking out motor rail services.

BY SEA
From Britain to northern Spain
Plymouth to Santander: **Brittany Ferries**, Millbay Docks, Plymouth PL1 3EW, tel: 0990 360360, fax: 01752 600698.

Portsmouth to Bilbao: **P&O European Ferries**, Peninsula House, Wharf Road, Portsmouth PO2 8TA, tel: 0990 980555, fax: 02392 864611.

From Málaga the scheduled Trasmediterránea service sails to Barcelona and the Canary Islands.

Getting Around

Most towns and villages are well served by bus and train, although the railway, the state-run RENFE organisation is not as comprehensive as the bus system. Some of the most attractive routes in the region (for example, Almería to Granada and Bobadilla to Málaga) can be covered easily by rail. Fares on RENFE are considerably cheaper than those in the UK. Although local trains that stop frequently may not keep too closely to timetables, Inter-city services are renowned for their punctuality.

BY BUS
The stretches between Málaga and Seville and between Ronda and Granada are particularly attractive ones to travel by road, and buses are a popular means of transport in Spain. They are reliable, low-priced, generally air conditioned, and offer a wide range of services. There are bus terminals in all the main towns and resorts.

BY CAR
International and local agencies will arrange for a car to be available at airports or other main holiday centres. Shortages can occur during peak season, so it is advisable to book your car in advance, either as part of a fly-drive package or through a travel agency (insist on fully comprehensive insurance). The hire firm will advise in case of a breakdown or accident. There are many local companies that often work out a lot cheaper.

CONNECTIONS
Almería
By air
Airport 9km (5 miles) from city centre on road to Níjar, tel: 950 21 37 41. Shuttlebus from Rambla del Obispo Orbera (near Plaza Purchena)
By train
Plaza de la Estación, tel: 950 25 11 35.
By bus
Plaza de Barcelona, tel: 950 21 00 29

Algeciras
By bus
Autobuses Portillo, Avenida Virgen del Carmen 15.
By boat
To Cueta, Melilla, Tangier and Canaries.

Córdoba
By train
Avenida de América for Madrid, Seville, Cádiz, Algeciras, Málaga, Granada and other destinations.
By bus
Main municipal terminus is in Plaza Tendillas. For Almería, Granada, Jaén, Málaga, Motril, Seville, and Madrid, Avenida Plaza de las Tres Culturas. Estación de Autobuses (behind the AVE station), tel: 957 40 40 40.

> **Railway treat**
> A special treat for train travellers is a journey in the old-fashioned luxury of **Al-Andalus**, which runs from Seville to Córdoba, Granada, Ronda and Jerez de la Frontera (April–October). For further information contact Al-Andalus Iberrail, Capitán Haya 55, Madrid 28020, tel: 915 715 815.

Granada

By air
Airport, 20km (12 miles) from Granada, tel: 957 47 12 27.

By train
Bobadilla station, Avenida de Andaluces, tel: 958 27 12 72.

By bus
Alsina Graells, Carretera de Jaén, tel: 958 18 50 10; Autédia Maestra,Carretera de Jaén, tel: 958 15 36 36.

Jaén

By train
Paseo de la Estación, tel: 953 25 56 07, for Almería, Granada, Córdoba, Madrid.

By bus
Plaza Coca de la Pinera, tel: 953 25 01 06, for Úbeda, Baeza, Cazorla, Madrid.

Málaga

By air
Pablo Ruiz Picasso Airport, 8km (5 miles) from the city centre, tel: 952 04 88 04. Bus to city centre (no 19).

By train
Cuarteles, tel: 952 36 02 02.

By bus
Paseo de los Tilos, tel: 952 35 00 61.

Seville

By air
Aeropuerta de San Pablo (by the NIV in the Córdoba direction), tel: 954 44 90 00.

By train
Estación de Santa Justa, Avenida Kansas City. All directions. Connection to AVE to Madrid, Córdoba.

By bus
Circular municipal bus services begin with 'C'. Main stops are Avenida Constitución, Plaza Nueva, Plaza de la Encarnación, Puerta de Jerez.
Bus station: Calle Manuel Vázquez Sagastizábal for Almería, Cádiz, Córdoba, Granada, Málaga, Ronda.

Facts for the Visitor

VISAS AND PASSPORTS

Citizens of Britain, the United States, Australia and New Zealand need a valid passport to enter Spain, while visitors from EU countries require only a valid national identity card. Visitors can prolong an automatic three-month stay by applying for an extension from a local *Oficina de Extranjeros* (Aliens Office) or police station.

CUSTOMS

Visitors from EU countries are not restricted in what they import as long as goods are not in commercial quantities. Non-EU nationals can import 200 cigarettes, 1 litre of spirits, 2 litres of wines and fortified wines, plus the usual personal effects. At Algeciras and Málaga in particular customs officials are eagle-eyed in their search for potential drug carriers.

TOURIST INFORMATION

The state-owned Spanish National Tourist Office will supply information to help with planning your holiday.

Public Holidays
1 January, 6 January (Epiphany), 28 February (Andalusia Day), 19 March (St Joseph's Day), Good Friday, 1 May (Labour Day), 25 July (St James' Day), 15 August (Feast of the Assumption), 12 October (National Day), 1 November (All Saints), 6 December (Constitution Day), 8 December (Immaculate Conception), 25 December (Christmas Day).

There are also a number of local holidays, celebrating the feast day of the parochial saint or Virgin. During these *ferias* normal commercial life often comes to a standstill. The huge Seville *feria*, and pre-Lent Carnival, particularly in Cádiz (see page 71), are difficult times to get anything serious accomplished.

ABROAD
Spanish National Tourist Office
In the UK
22–23 Manchester Square, London
W1M 5AP, tel: 0207 486 8077, fax:
0207 486 8034, brochure line: 9063
640 630, email: info.londres@tour-
spain.es, website: www.tourspain.
co.uk
In the US
666 Fifth Avenue, New York, NY
10103, tel: 212 265 8822, fax: 212 265
8864, email: nuevayork@tourspain.es,
website: www.okspain.org

IN SPAIN
These offices provide town maps and
other tourist material. The staff are
usually English-speaking.

Seville
Avda de la Constitución 21, tel: 954
22 14 04, fax: 954 22 97 53

Córdoba
Torrijos 10 (Palacio de Congresos y
Exposiciones), near La Mezquita, tel:
957 47 12 35, fax: 957 47 12 35.

Granada
Plaza Mariana Pineda 12 bajo, tel: 958
22 66 88.

Reading in the park

Almería
Parque N. Salmerón, tel: 950 27 43 35,
fax: 950 27 43 60.

Málaga
Pasaje de Chinitas 4, tel: 952 21 34 45,
and at the airport (terminal for international flights).

Cádiz
Calderón de la Barca 1, tel: 956 21 13 13.

Jerez de la Frontera
Alameda Cristina 7, tel: 956 33 11 50.

Jaén
Arquitecto Berges 1, tel: 953 22 27 37.

CURRENCY AND EXCHANGE
In February 2002, the Euro (EUR)
became the official currency used in
Spain. Notes are denominated in 5, 10,
20, 50, 100 and 500 Euros; coins in 1
and 2 Euros and 1, 2, 5, 10, 20 and 50
cents. Spanish coins of 1 and 2 Euros
depict King Juan Carlos I; the face of
Cervantes appears on the 10, 20 and
50 cent coins; and Santiago de Com-
postella Cathedral is shown on the 1,
2 and 5 cent coins.

The easiest way to obtain cash is
with a debit/credit card and a PIN number at one of the many ATM machines
(telebancos). Most shops and restau-

rants accept credit cards. For visitors from outside the Euro Zone, practically all Spanish banks will change foreign currency and travellers' cheques, but will charge a small commission. Rates can also vary from bank to bank and it is worth shopping around. There is no charge to change money at the Banco de España in Seville, Plaza San Francisco 17.

TIPPING

A 10 percent tip, or *propina,* is normal. In a bar or cafe it is usual to leave a few coins for the waiter. Chambermaids expect a sum appropriate to your length of stay; porters 2 Euros per item of luggage. When travelling by taxi, try to round up the fare.

OPENING TIMES

Shops usually open Monday–Friday 9.30am–1.30pm and 4.30–7/8pm, Saturday till 1pm. Food shops open a little earlier, supermarkets often stay open all day until 10pm.

Banks open Monday–Friday 8am–2pm, but *bureaux de change* have longer opening times, and also open sometimes on Saturday morning.

Post offices open Monday–Friday 9am–2pm, 4–6pm, Saturday morning.

Museums usually close all day on Monday, on Sunday afternoon and public holidays, plus weekdays from 1–4pm.

POST

Stamps *(sellos)* are available at tobacconists *(estancos)* and newsagents *(vendedor de periódicos).*

TELEPHONING

The code for Spain is 00 34. To dial the UK from Spain, prefix your number with 00 44 and omit the initial zero from the area code. The easiest way to make a phone call is to go to a *Telefónica* office where you make

your call and pay afterwards, but it is possible to make international calls from all public telephones. Phone cards *(tarjeta telefónica)* can be purchased at kiosks and tobacconists. Reduced tariffs for international calls apply from 10pm to 8am and all day Sunday. If you are using a US credit phone card, dial the company's access number below, then 01, and then the country code. Sprint tel: 900 99 0013; AT&T tel: 900 99 0011; MCI/Worldphone tel: 900 99 0014.

All Spanish subscribers now have nine-digit numbers. The first three digits are the former provincial area code.

NEWSPAPERS AND MAGAZINES

Newsagents always keep a good supply of English newspapers; some even have an edition printed in Spain. A

Gifts and souvenirs

Things to look out for in Andalusia include embroidered *mantillas* and genuine flamenco dancing shoes. You will also find painted fans and horn combs, finely cut jewellery and a variety of pottery. Baskets woven from *esparto* grass and *alpargatas,* shoes of the same material, are sold in Almería.

Córdoba's Asociación Cordobesa de Artesanos, in the Zoco Municipal, specialises in traditional crafts. Look out for leather goods in Meryan workshops in Callejón de las Flores.

In Granada go to Artespaña, in the Corral del Carbón, for traditional craftwork. Mariana Pineda on Cuesta de Gomérez is a long-established guitar-making workshop.

Málaga is an excellent place for pottery. Alquimia Cerámica, Alamos 45, sells bowls, amphoras and jugs in natural, antique-effect colours. Alfamare in Calle Antillas also specialise in classic shapes in earthy shades.

Seville's traffic-free Calle Sierpes is a shopper's paradise. Goods include hand-painted fans, mantillas, porcelain and leather goods.

range of periodicals and magazines are produced for English expatriates, containing useful 'what's on' sections. *Lookout*, a glossy monthly, is the most respected. *Sur*, Málaga's daily newspaper in Spanish, publishes a free edition in English every Friday.

TIME
Spain is one hour ahead of Greenwich Mean Time (GMT +1). Summer time (GMT + 2) lasts from late March until the last Sunday in September.

VOLTAGE
This is usually 220V AC, although in some rural areas the voltage is still 110V. A continental adaptor is essential for visitors from Britain.

THE DISABLED
The Spanish National Tourist Office *(see page 120)* publishes a fact sheet, listing useful addresses and details of some accessible accommodation. The **Oficina de Turismo para Personas Decapacitadas**, Calle Patrizio Sáenz 7, Seville, tel: 952 438 66 45, can supply general information on facilities.

CLOTHING
You may feel a little conspicuous wearing brief shorts or shoulder-baring tops in towns and larger centres. When visiting churches, wear discreet, respectable clothing. Spaniards like to dress up when going out in the evening but most restaurants don't have a dress code. In the spring and autumn it can get quite cool at night, particularly in Granada and in the Alpujarras, so remember to pack something warm.

MEDICAL ASSISTANCE
If an emergency arises, go to the accident and emergency department of a hospital or summon help by dialling 091. If the need is less urgent, ask at your hotel or tourist office for the address of the nearest health centre *(centro de salud)* or the name of a doctor, preferably English-speaking.

Although travellers from EU countries are advised to acquire the E111 certificate, which entitles holders to take advantage of health facilities in any EU country free of charge, it is wise to have an accident and illness insurance policy as well. Make sure you get a detailed invoice *(factura)* to present to your insurance company.

A green cross on a white background signifies a chemist *(farmacia)*. Pharmacists are highly trained and can dispense many drugs that would be available only on prescription in the UK. Emergency opening times are published in daily newspapers.

Emergencies
For police, fire brigade and ambulance, tel: 091.

CRIME
It is important to take what precautions you can to prevent car break-ins and theft, particularly in the main tourist centres. Never leave anything of value in the car and always keep the boot locked. Larger quantities of money and valuable jewellery should be stored in the hotel safe. Take special care of property in crowded areas such as markets. Notify the police if you are the victim of theft, as your insurance company will need written confirmation.

DIPLOMATIC REPRESENTATION
British Consulates: Plaza Nueva 8, Seville, tel: 954 22 88 75; Edificio Duquesa, Calle Duquesa de Parcent 8, 29001 Málaga, tel: 952 21 75 71, fax: 952 22 11 30.
American Consulates: Paseo Deliciás 7, Seville, tel: 954 23 18 85; Centro Comercial Las Rampas, Phase 2, 1, Fuengirola, tel: 952 47 48 91.

ACCOMMODATION

Parador, fonda, hostal – the range of accommodation in Spain can be confusing. As elsewhere, hotels are classified with one to five stars according to the facilities provided. There are also the more basic *hostales,* which have an **H** sign outside; **HR** indicates that there is no restaurant. The *pensión, fonda* (inn) and *casa de huéspedes* (guest house) offer inexpensive, simple types of accommodation.

Spanish hotel owners are obliged to display in every room a price list showing seasonal adjustments, additional bed supplements and the cost of breakfast *(desayuno)* and half and full board *(media pensión, pensión completa).* It must also be clearly shown whether VAT (IVA) is included in the price.

HOLIDAYS IN THE COUNTRYSIDE

Families and nature lovers often like to rent a holiday apartment or a villa in the countryside *(casa rural).* If you choose this type of accommodation, you will almost certainly need a car.

Hoteles Rurales, country hotels, offer an informal atmosphere, traditional gastronomy, a quiet location and special activities, e.g. riding holidays. The Spanish National Tourist Office *(see page 120)* supply brochures or you could also contact **Asociación de Hoteles Rurales de Andalucía,** Sagunto 8, E-04004 Almería, tel: 950 26 50 18, fax: 950 27 04 31.

Another alternative is offered by the **Red Andaluza de Alojamientos Rurales** (www.raar.es). This organisation, based in Almería, provides a wide range of accommodation in rural areas: anything from Arab-inspired tents to traditional *fincas* in fruit orchards or smart, rustic-style hotels with swimming pools, all in remote mountain regions. Contact them at

RAAR, Apartado de Correos, 2035, E-04080 Almería, tel: 950 26 50 18, fax: 950 27 04 31.

A relatively new amenity are the government-run **Villas Turísticas,** free-standing dwellings in scenic mountain locations. These self-catering apartments can be rented in holiday villages such as Bubión, Cazalla de la Sierra and Cazorla.

YOUTH HOSTELS

A directory of youth hostels in Spain is available from the Spanish National Tourist Office *(see page 120)*, or contact the National Youth Hostel Association, 8 St Stephen's Hill, St Albans, Herts AL1 2DY, tel: 0870 870 8808; fax: 01727 844126. Generally speaking, however, Spanish *fondas* and the more basic *hostales* are in the same price range as youth hostels.

CAMPING

There are many well-equipped campsites in Andalusia, mostly by the coast. Camping is also permitted in the nature reserves. The Spanish National Tourist Office has all the details and good bookshops keep a range of the guides listing international campsites.

Paradores

The *Paradores Nacionales* are a chain of state-run hotels with a long tradition, in many cases occupying historic buildings, but always in fine settings and furnished in local style. Andalusia has 18 such hotels, some of which rank as the finest in Spain (Jaén, Úbeda, Carmona, Granada, Málaga, Ronda, and Arcos de la Frontera). Reservations and information: Central Reservation Office for Paradors in Spain, Calle Requena 3, 28013 Madrid, tel: 915 16 666, fax: 915 16 657; website: www.parador.es.

Hotel Selection

These suggestions for hotels in Andalusia are listed according to the following categories: $$$= expensive; $$= moderate; $= inexpensive.

Cádiz

Atlántico, Duque de Nájera 9, tel: 956 22 69 05, fax: 956 21 45 82. Nice location in the Parque de Genovés. The most stylish hotel in Cádiz. $$$.

Francia y París, Plaza San Francisco 2, tel: 956 22 23 48, fax: 956 22 24 31. Quiet hotel in an historic setting. $$.

Imares, San Francisco 9, tel: 956 21 22 57. A well-maintained hotel. $.

Córdoba

Amistad Córdoba, Plaza de Maimónides 3, tel: 957 42 03 35, fax: 957 42 03 65. Two former mansions in the Judería. Tastefully furnished, plus an excellent restaurant. $$$.

Alfaros, Alfaros 18, tel: 957 49 19 20. Modern hotel in an old building. Andalusian-style furnishing. $$.

González, Manríquez 3, tel: 957 47 98 19, fax: 957 48 61 87. A fine 16th-century mansion in the Judería quarter. $$.

El Califa, Lope de Hoces, tel: 957 29 94 00, fax: 957 29 57 16. Traditional, but modern hotel with patio. Near the mosque. $$.

El Triunfo, Corregidor Luis de la Cerdá 79, tel: 957 47 55 00, fax: 957 48 68 50. Informal , at the rear of the mosque. $$.

Selu, Eduardo Dato 7, tel: 957 47 65 00. Modern, inner-city hotel. $.

Hostal Los Arcos, Romero Barros, tel: 957 48 56 43, fax: 957 48 60 11. Round the corner from pretty Plaza del Potro. Popular with backpackers. $.

Alcázar, San Basilio 2, tel: 957 20 25 61. Basic. Near the Jardines de Campo Santo. $

Marisa, Cardenal Herrero 6, tel: 957 47 31 42. Comfortable, friendly. $

Granada

Alhambra Palace, Peña Partida 2, tel: 958 22 14 68, fax: 958 22 64 04. Luxury hotel by the Alameda, opposite the Alhambra, with a magnificent view over the town. Delightful tea-rooms, terraces; elegant rooms. $$$.

Parador San Francisco, Alhambra, tel: 958 22 14 40, fax: 958 22 22 64. One of the most delightful *paradores* in a converted Franciscan monastery, with terrace adjoining the Alhambra. Only 35 rooms, so reservations months in advance are essential. $$$.

Dauro II, Navas 5, tel: 958 22 15 81, fax: 958 22 27 32. An elegant, well-maintained hotel in the pedestrian zone. 48 rooms. $$.

Washington Irving, Generalife 2, tel: 958 22 75 50, fax: 958 22 88 40. In the shade of the Alhambra. Has the faded splendour of a once-grand hotel. Large rooms; kitschy dining room. $$.

Málaga

Parador de Gibralfaro, tel: 952 22 19 02, fax: 952 22 19 04. Rustic *parador* in woods above Málaga. Only 12 rooms; advance booking essential. Magnificent view of the city. $$$.

Málaga Palacio, Cortina del Muelle, tel: 952 21 51 85, fax: 952 22 25 100. Modern, comfortable block in the city centre. Great view over the cathedral and Alcazaba from the roof terrace (with swimming pool). $$$.

Don Curro, Sancha de Lara 7, tel: 952 22 72 00. Lots of wood and velvet in classical style. Smallish rooms, but central location. $$.

Lis, Córdoba 7, tel: 952 22 73 00, fax: 952 22 73 09. Basic but comfortable accommodation. $

Seville

Alfonso XIII, San Fernando 2, tel: 954 22 28 50, fax: 954 21 60 33. The finest and plushest hotel in Seville. Gardens and swimming pool. $$$.

Doña María, Don Remondo 19, tel: 954 22 49 90, fax: 954 21 95 46. Very close to the cathedral in a former mansion. Swimming pool. $$$.

Los Seises, Segovias 6, tel: 954 22 94 95, fax: 954 22 43 34. From the rooftop swimming pool, the Giralda is so close you can almost touch it. Modern, but elegant. $$$.

Hostería del Laurel, Plaza de los Venerables 5, tel: 954 22 02 95, fax: 954 21 04 50. In the heart of the Barrio Santa Cruz, near the Laurel bar. $$.

Hostal Goya, Mateos Gago 31, tel: 954 21 11 70, fax: 954 56 29 88. Comfortable, quiet, central location. $$.

Simón, García de Vinuesa 19, tel: 954 22 66 60, fax: 954 56 22 41. Near the cathedral. Very good value in attractive 18th-century patio-style house. $.

Zaida, San Roque 26, tel: 954 21 11 38. Small, smart hotel near the Museo de Bellas Artes. $.

Alhama de Granada

Balneario Alhama de Granada, tel: 958 35 00 11, fax: 958 35 02 97. The remains of a Moorish bath have been integrated into a new spa hotel. About 3km (2 miles) from town centre. $$.

Baño Nuevo, tel: 958 35 00 11. A less expensive option to the adjoining the Balneario Alhama de Granada. $.

Antequera

Parador de Antequera, García del Olmo, tel: 952 84 02 61, fax: 952 84 13 12. Modern, with a pool. $$.

Las Pedrizas, Ctra Madrid–Málaga Km 527, tel: 952 73 08 50, fax: 952 73 08 52. Well-equipped; suitable for the disabled. $$

La Yedra, Ctra Córdoba–Málaga, tel: 952 84 22 87. Basic, well-positioned hotel with cafeteria. $.

Arcos de la Frontera

Parador Casa del Corregidor, Plaza del Cabildo, tel: 956 70 05 00, fax: 956 70 11 16. Splendid location, delightful patio, impressive view. $$$.

Los Olivos, San Miguel 2, tel: 956 70 08 11, fax: 956 70 20 18. Attractive hotel in an old mansion. $$.

Baeza

Baeza, Concepción 3, tel: 953 74 81 30, fax: 953 74 25 19. All modern conveniences in a restored hospital building. $$.

Bailén

Parador, Avenida de Málaga, tel: 953 67 01 00, fax: 953 67 25 30. On the edge of town; 1960s-style; functional and comfortable. $$.

Cuatro Caminos, Sebastián Elcano 34, tel: 953 67 02 19, fax: 953 67 30 38. Small hotel with 22 rooms. $.

Carmona

Parador Alcázar del Rey Don Pedro, tel: 954 14 10 10, fax: 954 14 17 12. Medieval atmosphere and great view of Carmona. $$$.

Cazorla

Andalucía, Martínez Falero 42, tel: 953 72 12 68. A good, comfortable hotel, but it has no restaurant. $

Don Diego, Hilario Marcos 163, tel: 953 72 05 31. Another good-value hotel without its own restaurant. $

Jaén

Parador Castillo de Santa Catalina, Castillo de Santa Catalina, tel: 953 23 00 00, fax: 953 23 09 30. A modern *parador* in the grounds of the old castle, adapted to suit the medieval architecture. $$$.

Xauen, Plaza de Dean Mazas, tel: 953 24 07 89, fax: 953 19 03 12. Near Plaza de la Constitución. Smart town-centre hotel, stylishly furnished. $$.

Reyes Católicos, Avenida de Granada 1, tel/fax: 953 22 22 50. Friendly, and has a cafeteria. $.

Jerez de la Frontera

Jerez, Avenida Alvaro Domecq 35, tel: 956 30 06 00, fax: 956 30 50 01. Modern, spacious hotel with swimming pool and tennis courts. $$$.

Royal Sherry Park, Alvaro Domecq 11, tel: 956 30 30 11, fax: 956 31 13 00. Luxurious hotel with pool. $$$.

San Miguel, San Miguel 4, tel: 956 34 85 62. Pleasant and inexpensive. $.

Lanjarón

Miramar, Avenida Andalucía 10, tel: 958 77 01 61. The best-equipped hotel in the town. $$.

Andalucía, Avenida Andalucía 15, tel: 958 77 01 36. Central location. $.

Loja

El Mirador, Carretera Jerez–Cartagena Km 485, tel: 958 32 00 42, fax: 958 32 06 35. Picturesque setting. $.

Nerja

Parador de Nerja, Almuñécar 8, tel: 952 52 00 50, fax: 952 52 19 97. Large gardens and swimming pool. $$$.

Ronda

Parador de Ronda, Plaza España, tel: 952 87 75 00, fax: 952 87 71 88. A new, ultra-modern *parador* in the former town hall. $$$.

Reina Victoria, Jérez 25, tel: 952 87 12 40, fax: 952 87 10 75. Faithfully classical style, attractive garden, idyllic view. $$$.

Don Miguel, Villanueva 8, tel: 952 87 77 22, fax: 952 87 83 77. Unbeatable position on the precipice above the Río Guadalevín. Terraced restaurant. $$.

Polo, Mariano Soubirón 8, tel: 952 87 24 47, fax: 952 87 24 49. Small, bright and modern. $.

Sanlúcar de Barrameda

Tartaneros, Tartaneros 8, tel: 956 36 20 44, fax: 956 36 00 45. A mansion in the older quarter of the town. $$.

Posada de Palacio, Caballero 11, tel: 956 36 48 40, fax: 956 36 50 60. Small hotel in a patio-style house. $.

Sierra de Cazorla

Parador El Adelantado, tel/fax: 953 72 10 75. Luxury hotel in a remote location in the forest. $$$.

Noguera de la Sierpe, Carretera del Tranco Km15, tel/fax: 953 71 30 21. A good starting points for walking tours in the region. $$.

Río, Carretera del Tranco Km8, tel: 953 71 30 73, fax: 953 71 30 35. Also ideal for walkers. $.

Tarifa

Balcón de España, Carretera Cádiz–Málaga Km 77, tel/fax: 956 68 43 26. Garden, swimming pool and tennis courts. $$.

Dos Mares, Carretera Cádiz Km 79, tel: 956 68 40 35, fax: 956 68 10 78. Stylishly furnished; popular beach restaurant; swimming pool, tennis court; surfing and riding holidays. $$.

Hostal Alameda, Santísima Trinidad 7, tel: 956 68 11 81. Small, clean and airy hotel. $.

La Alborada, San José 52, tel: 956 68 11 40, fax: 956 68 19 35. Clean and functional. Breakfast bar. $.

Úbeda

Parador Nacional del Condestable Dávalos, Plaza de Vázquez Molina 1, tel: 953 75 03 45, fax: 953 75 12 59. Housed in a restored 16th-century palace. Splendid patio. $$.

La Paz, Andalucía 1, tel: 953 75 21 46, fax: 953 75 08 48. Very comfortable; delicious regional food. $.

Vejer de la Frontera

Convento San Francisco, Plazuela, tel: 956 45 10 01, fax: 956 45 10 04. In a former monastery. Dining room with interesting frescoes. Excellent meals and wine menu to match. $$.

✥ INSIGHT COMPACT GUIDES

Great Little Guides to the following destinations:

Algarve	Goa	St Petersburg	North York Moors
Amsterdam	Gran Canaria	Salzburg	Northumbria
Athens	Greece	Shanghai	Oxford
Bahamas	Holland	Singapore	Peak District
Bali	Hong Kong	Southern Spain	Scotland
Bangkok	Ibiza	Sri Lanka	Scottish
Barbados	Iceland	Switzerland	Highlands
Barcelona	Ireland	Sydney	Shakespeare
Beijing	Israel	Tenerife	Country
Belgium	Italian Lakes	Thailand	Snowdonia
Berlin	Italian Riviera	Toronto	South Downs
Bermuda	Jamaica	Turkey	York
Brittany	Jerusalem	Turkish Coast	Yorkshire Dales
Bruges	Kenya	Tuscany	
Brussels	Laos	Venice	*USA regional*
Budapest	Lisbon	Vienna	*titles:*
Burgundy	Madeira	Vietnam	Boston
California	Madrid	West of Ireland	Cape Cod
Cambodia	Mallorca		Chicago
Chile	Malta	*UK regional*	Florida
Copenhagen	Menorca	*titles:*	Florida Keys
Costa Brava	Milan	Bath &	Hawaii – Maui
Costa del Sol	Montreal	Surroundings	Hawaii – Oahu
Costa Rica	Morocco	Belfast	Las Vegas
Crete	Moscow	Cambridge &	Los Angeles
Cuba	Munich	East Anglia	Martha's Vineyard
Cyprus	Normandy	Cornwall	& Nantucket
Czech Republic	Norway	Cotswolds	Miami
Denmark	Paris	Devon & Exmoor	New Orleans
Dominican	Poland	Edinburgh	New York
Republic	Portugal	Glasgow	San Diego
Dublin	Prague	Guernsey	San Francisco
Egypt	Provence	Jersey	Washington DC
Finland	Rhodes	Lake District	
Florence	Rio de Janeiro	London	
French Riviera	Rome	New Forest	

Insight's checklist to meet all your travel needs:

- **Insight Guides** provide the complete picture, with expert cultural background and stunning photography. Great for travel planning, for use on the spot, and as a souvenir. 180 titles.
- **Insight Pocket Guides** focus on the best choices for places to see and things to do, picked by our correspondents. They include large fold-out maps. More than 120 titles.
- **Insight Compact Guides** are fact-packed books to carry with you for easy reference when you're on the move in a destination. More than 130 titles.
- **Insight Maps** combine clear, detailed cartography with essential information and a laminated finish that makes the maps durable and easy to fold. 125 titles.
- **Insight Phrasebooks** and **Insight Travel Dictionaries** are very portable and help you find exactly the right word in French, German, Italian and Spanish.

The world's largest collection of visual travel guides and maps

INDEX

Alcalá de
    Guadaira 87
Alcalá la Real 83
Algeciras 68–9
Alhama de
    Granada. 61
Almería 58–60
    Alcazaba 59
Almuñécar.......60, 94
Alpujarras 94
Antequera 85–6
Aracena ....:........37
Archidona 85
architecture 103–6
Arcos de la
    Frontera 79
art 103–6
azulejos 27, 104
Baena 84
Baeza.................98–9
Bahía de Cádiz 71
Bailén 93
Baroque 105
Barrio de Santiago 82
Benalmádena.........64
bodegas 88
Bosque (El) 78
Brenan, Gerald 96
Bubión.................95
bullfighting ..16–7, 77
Cádiz 71–4
Calahorra (La).......82
camping...............123
Capileira 95
Carlota (La)...........93
Carmona 91–2
cave dwellings...82–3
Cazorla 101
Churriguerismo...105
climate.................8–9
cofradías 110
Córdoba...........38–45
    Alcázar de los Reyes
        Cristianos 43
    history.................38
    Jewish Quarter.41–2
    Mezquita.39–41, 103
    Synagogue 42
cortijos 104
Costa de la Luz 70
Costa del Sol 58–65
customs 119

Drake, Sir Francis ..72
drinks 114
Ecija 92–3
Embalse Tranco
    de Beas 101
Espejo 84
Estepona 65
Festivals 109–10
flamenco ...15–6, 108
food 113
Fortaleza
    de la Mota...........83
Fuengirola 64
Fuente Vaqueros 84
Garganta
    del Chorro...........86
Gibralfaro 62
Gibraltar 66–8
gitanos...........14–5, 87
Golden Age 107
golf 116
Granada...........47–57
    Albaicín 56
    Alhambra.48–53, 104
        Generalife 53
    Capilla Real 55
    Catedral 55
    history.................47
    Monasterio
        de la Cartuja......57
    Sacramonte 56
Grazalema 78
Gruta de las
    Maravillas...........37
Guadix...............82–3
History 18–9
hotels 124–6
Iruela (La) 101
Irving,
    Washington....49, 52
Itálica 35
Jaen 97–8
Jerez de
    la Frontera 88
Language 69
Lanjarón 94
Lebrija.................90
literature 106–8
Loja 85
Lorca, Federico
    García 84–5, 107
Lucena.................84

Madinat al-Zahra ..46
Málaga 61–3
    Semana Santa 111
Marbella 64–5
Medina Sidonia..70–1
Mini-Hollywood ...60
Moguer 36
Monasterio
    de la Rábida 36
Morocco 68
Mudéjares 103
Nerja.................60
Niebla 36
Olvera.................77–8
Orgiva 95
Osuna 87
Palos de la
    Frontera 36
Palma del Río 46
Pampaneira 95
Paradores 123
Parque Nacional Coto
    de Doñana...11, 36
Parque Natural
    de la Sierra de
        Grazalema 78–9
Parque Natural Sierras
    de Cazorla, Segura
        y las Villas ..100–1
Parque Natural
    del Torcal 86–7
passports 119
Picasso Foundation.62
plateresque 24, 79
Priego de Córdoba.84
public holidays 119
pueblos
    blancos 70, 75–9
Puerto Banús.........65
Puerto de la Mora ..83
Puerto de
    Santa María ..74, 90
Puerto del Suspiro
    del Moro...........96
Punta Marroquí 70
Purullena.............83
Restaurants 114–5
riding.................116
Rocío (El) 36
Romanticism........107
Ronda 75–7
rural tourism 11

Salobreña 60
San Pedro de
    Alcántara 65
Sanlúcar de
    Barrameda 74
Santa Fé 84
Santa María de la
    Defensión 90
Semana Santa 110–11
Setenil 77
sevillana 108–9
Seville 23–35
    Casa de Pilatos 33
    Catedral 24–6
    Giralda 25, 104
    history.................23
    Hospital de la
        Caridad.............31
    Isla Májica 29
    Jewish Quarter 28
    Macarena (La) 35
    Museo de
        Bellas Artes 34
    Royal Palace 26–8
Semana
    Santa 23, 111
sherry 12, 114
Sierra de
    Alhamilla 60
Sierra de Almijara..61
Sierra de Aracena ..37
Sierra
    Nevada 8–10, 94
sports.................116
Tajo (El) 75
tapas 113
Tarifa.................69–70
Torre del Mar........61
Torremolinos.........64
Trevélez 95–6
Ubeda 99–100
Ubrique 78
Ugíjar 96
Vejer de la
    Frontera 70
Velázquez, Diego..105
Vélez Málaga 61
verdiales 108
Walking 116
wines 114
Yegen 96
youth hostels 123